marini

marini

Alberto Busignani

Hamlyn
London   New York   Sydney   Toronto

twentieth-century masters
General editors: H. L. Jaffé and A. Busignani

© Copyright in the text Sadea/Sansoni Florence 1968
Photographs: Liberto Perugi
© Copyright this edition The Hamlyn Publishing Group Limited 1971
London · New York · Sydney · Toronto
Hamlyn House, Feltham, Middlesex, England
ISBN 0 600 35927 1

Colour lithography: Zincotipia Moderna, Florence
Printed and bound in England by Cox and Wyman Limited,
London, Fakenham and Reading

Distributed in the United States of America by Crown Publishers Inc.

contents

List of colour illustrations

List of black-and-white illustrations

Myth: meaning and value

Marino Marini, sculptor of horses and Pomonas, of miracles and portraits may be described as the sculptor of myths and the poet of a remote humanity; for he exposes the very roots of existence in the intangible absoluteness of the forms he creates with such primordial potency and weight. This continuous connection of Marini's with myth, however, is likely to encourage the critic to make allusions, especially to antiquity, in order to explain the great fascination his sculpture has for us. Discussion of his work has been couched not in critical terms but in such unashamedly poetic ones as 'the smile of the Etruscans', or as evocations of the Gothic and medieval. But Umbro Apollonio comments: 'This great artist always offers us a situation both ancient and modern, open to varied references in the historical field but always set, without query, in the vital thrust of a universal uplift in which all our uncertainties and aspirations find expression at one and the same time.' We might clarify this concept of the myth by saying that in contemporary culture the resort to myth indicates a rejection not so much of reality as of contingency; the rejection, in other words, of a way of living judged to be negative, valueless instead of valuable. Resorting to myth infers abstraction into a world of ideas which have an absolute aesthetic validity; a validity that in relation to reality assumes a symbolic value. Myth, in other words, is the symbol of existence, of life itself, and its essential meaning is beyond the contingent occurrence of events.

Naturally, if art is considered an ethical and political function, and not only a lyrical expression of feeling, an attitude of resorting to myth may seem in a way, renunciatory. Certainly its most striking facet, that of avoiding treatment of the concrete, daily occurrence of reality, might lead one to form largely negative opinions of it, to consider it, when all is said and done, a purely formal position admitting of no problems. But we must also see whether, by propounding a mythical world in which good and evil figure through symbols that have an absolute value, the myth itself does not inveigh into reality by direct intervention; and whether, if it does, the work of art acquires a powerful moral significance. Here it is necessary to distinguish between 'myth' and 'fetish'. Fetish, in fact, is mainly connected in contemporary society, with contingency; it is the symbol, the provocative questioning of values which our society has endowed with falsely positive significance. Pop art, which arises in a society such as that of America which has reached the highest possible material standard of living gains its validity precisely through fetishes, endowing them with a violently corrosive power, and making them ironic symbols of values held to be positive, but which are basically negative, such as one particular type of

The incidence of myth into reality

well-being, one particular form of social organisation and so on. The hot-dog reproduced larger than life by a Pop artist has, or may have, exactly this meaning, a mixture of provocation and dispute.

Myth, on the other hand, though perhaps born out of the same social situation, does not appear as a provocative symbol or a furious criticism, but as a positive act of choice. This establishes a reality in art which we often define ideal, in the sense that it separates out of the totality of the real the individual expression of that totality. Thus it propounds the poetic model of an absolute reality that has absolute values.

Myth, then, is nothing to do with the far-off, fairy-tale visions of fantasy, but is a judgment of reality. This is particularly and most evidently true in artists who are outstandingly rationalistic, like Mondrian, and expound the myth of the rationality of the real in an art of typically normative character; an art, that is, which claims to offer itself as the model to which reality should liken itself.

Setting aside our contemporaries for the moment, it is clear that the art-myth analogy applies most of all to works we call archaic; and that these appear so to us not so much by their early place in the parabola of progress to which traditional criticism has accustomed us, as because they actually lacked awareness of the essential substratum of which they were functions. The *Hera of Samos* with her columnar power grooved by the folds of her chiton and wonderfully headless, and the Doric maidens with their divine smiles, these are all myth to us since archaeological criticism has never yet been able to formulate a plan of enquiry to explain their innermost relation with existence. In other words, these works are related to a world of fable which is irretrievably lost in time past, and just for that reason strangely fascinating. In cases like these, the concept of myth is something we superimpose on a reality which can only be partially sounded.

Myth as relative and absolute in history

Diversely, when treated as a historical subject, myth has been used as a term relating to an ideal in many phases of the evolution of artistic ideas. Myth was the idea of the classical in a continuous tradition from Petrarch to the early Renaissance, and – because of its innate capacity for promoting ideals – in the French neo-classical revolution.

Contemporary artists have rejected the historic connection (at least since Gauguin: the myth of the exotic as a lost paradise which is retrievable only in a world of actions and feelings falsely called primitive; or Douanier Rousseau: myth as a childlike, naïve region of the soul). One might, then, credit all that work of our contemporaries which avoids direct dispute about reality with a basic unconcern for query, and contrast the art of 'incidence' (such as Picasso's *Guernica*) with one of fable and non-allegory (such as Picasso's unhistorical neo-classicism). And here we are back to the idea with which we began, the meaning of myth as it affects creation and expression.

We have said above that almost the whole of contingency is rejected; which involves a judgment and therefore sets up a query. If the values of existence are actually non-values, the thunderous brilliance of a *Miracle* by Marini must appear no less valid ethically than the violent, fierce condemnation of *Guernica*.

Thus, then, the refutation of contingency, and the negative aspects of being, are vindicated in the affirmation that being itself is positive. Myth finds its justification not as fable, as a point of flight from reality, but as a synthesis of values, like an alternative argument with an eternal validity. Materially it shows itself to be an interpretation of history just by its apparent absoluteness.

Thus far it seems clear that as far as its relation to the past is concerned, myth in contemporary art may have regained the existential significance which it had in antiquity (utterly different from that historical sense of the classical ideal which it had from the thirteenth to the eighteenth centuries and which we have already referred to). But it has regained this significance

through different channels: I was going to say through lack of faith instead of by faith. In antiquity if the creation of myth answered some idealisation of reality, in which contingency came naturally to have some validity (myth as an affirmation of the divine), nowadays it stands as a perception of values against the acknowledgment of false values, a selection from reality instead of an infinite acceptance of it.

This schematic framework and attempt to pinpoint a matter which constitutes one of the major features of contemporary art seems to me to be essential, not only to remind us of ethical order but to clarify the artist's relation to reality and his implicit judgment.

The theme of myth as a perception of total truth

We have quoted above 'the smile of the Etruscans' as a metaphor intended to define, by what I might call intuitive analogy, a constant quality in the sculpture of Marini. This quality is an earthiness blended with the remote solemnity of a timeless ideal. But if, in a list of the cultural influences felt by the sculptor, who is moreover Tuscan, the presence of Etruscan art is discounted, it remains to be seen whether there are clear signs of other elements which apparently have their roots in some hypothetical and possibly ethnic consciousness, as with Arnolfo, Donatello, or even Michelangelo.

A purely formal analysis, therefore, at the beginning of our quest—is useless. It could only at best establish the means of a connection, without ascertaining its reasons; that is to say, its substance and very being. What matters is to specify how the Etruscan world can constitute a point of ideal reference for Marino, involving—mythically and not historically—a range of existential values which he considers absolutely pre-eminent. Obviously we are dealing with a world out of time (mythical and not historical) within which the urgency of everyday reality eventually establishes itself through an intimate vital exchange. More precisely, we are dealing with the hypothesis of a sphere of existence and thence of forms, determined by analogy, from Marino's own existential sphere. Most probably the historical Etruscans, seen in the proper context and formal structure of their times, are far from being those fairy-tale Etruscans whom too many have helped to create. But they are the vision of our poetic intuition, and not our critical analysis, of that mythical, ancient world.

Thus, then, there are two forms of reconstruction of the past. One is historical; which is the task of the historian and philologist. The other is quite different, basically intuitive and mythical (by which Marino becomes 'Etruscan' or 'Egyptian' and Picasso 'neo-classical' or 'negro') and aims to define one's own emotions and psychological receptions when faced with a work of art capable of an eternal message.[1]

Returning to Marino's relations with the Etruscan world, criticism probably dwells on them with a certain insistence principally for ethnic reasons (as it has done, and with far less good sense, with another Tuscan, namely Campigli). In fact the Marinian myth can be similarly related to other expressions of events by Egyptian (and why not Sumerian too) or Roman sculptors. The *Saint Martin and the Poor Man* in Lucca Cathedral offers a splendid pretext for pseudo philology basically because of its subject: almost a kind of *Horse and Rider* before their time. In reality any work of his we refer to reveals moments in which the raw essence of mankind and the inert weight of matter in which the sculpture is created (with powerful effect and binding solemnity) have combined to produce summary, gigantic definitions, simplifications and measurements of immediate significance;

---

1 It is interesting to note Toesca's austere admonition 'First connoisseurs and then historians' (which should be understood as a recall to the matter of problems and away from general theorising, for there is no knowledge without history; and yet we must be historians to be connoisseurs). Longhi quotes this as authoritative; and it may indeed have brought forth a crop of experts but it has not prevented any one of them from boringly indulging in the literature and landscape of criticism. So much so that the rottenest fruits of decadence should be looked for among art critics before all others. On the other hand, when a connoisseur understands his role as that of recognising aesthetic value (in other words, of asserting a quality—itself hypothetical) he can only give an account of his personal, psychological and emotional, relationship with it. And this is reflected, of course, in the literature, both the good and the not so good.

an expression of life without intermediary. Not that other artists of other epochs (we have already referred to Donatello and Michelangelo) have not revealed equal urgency, but between them and Marini a historical gauze seems to have been interposed, a cultural filter, even a habit of intellect which has set them all in a critical not intuitive relation, in time and not outside it. But his archaic subjects on the other hand, have the appearance of life itself, in its own process of coming-to-be; of myth, and not history.

2. *The People*
1929, terracotta, only copy
base 43 × 18½ in (109 × 47 cm)
height 26 in (66 cm)
Property of the artist,
Milan

So it is not the Etruscan, the Egyptian or Roman masters, but a perception of total truth, of man's simple and solemn presence in being, that stands at the root of Marini's eternal antiquity and his various formal interpretations of it. And this permeates and justifies the creation of the myth as an absolutely valid affirmation.

If this discussion deals with the posing of general questions and is reviewed here as a preliminary to putting Marini in the best historical context to understand his aesthetic, it nonetheless receives necessary confirmation from a more detailed analysis of the facts. Indeed it receives it from the very start, from the moment in which his work manifests itself beyond personal pre-history. Let us take *The People* of 1929 to be number one, chronologically, in the Marinian œuvre for its synthesis of themes which thenceforward recur repeatedly, in a much more finished sense than the barely perceptible implications in his works of the preceding year: *The Sick Woman, The Blind Man, Cristina*. This work, over and beyond its immediate cultural allusions (the sarcophagi of Chiusi, Cerveteri and Cere, or even more incisively, the burial urns of Volterra), represents the evaluation of a reality which makes claims on eternity, as its somewhat programmatic title suggests. However rightly one insists upon 'the typically popular character that the artist took in his early works from his Tuscan and Etruscan heritage'[2] (Carandente), the beginnings of Marino will not be understood unless we perceive in them the need to uncover an original layer of existence, and to seize and immediately transfer urgency of being into a symbolic absolute (or myth). In doing this we have to dispense with the recital of his cultural and formal apprenticeship. Here are no historical Etruscans but a perception of total truth. Urns and canopies, which are the basic inspiration of *The People*, must have represented a concrete, earthy reality more authentic

**Symbolic absolute
and ethical judgment**

Fig. 2

2 G. Carandente: Introduction to the *Catalogue* of the Marino Marini exhibition, Rome 1966.

than Rodin or Maillol, with which to counteract the twentieth-century academic exercises Italian art was tending towards. This is sufficiently proved by the fact that a choice of this kind, the choice of so vulgar a humanity, itself advances the maintenance of a truth in which an initial ethical judgment is implicit. His fundamental reality is not so much Rousseauesque as, I should say, Marxian.[3] Certainly this title, *The People*, tends to transfer a vulgar character from the two exceptionally potent symbol-protagonists of Marino's sculpture to all those concrete Etruscan shapes from Volterra and Chiusi.

But because of this basic character, we ought perhaps to classify this work as popular rather than vulgar ('of the people'). It may then reflect as much as one wishes of 'typical' character, which is both positive and real, but it will also show that Marini's thought lies within a sphere of native, if not utterly naïve, good humour. It is popular by the universality of its choice (a real that is 'the real': a single manifestation becomes the embodiment of aspirations and experiences to which we are likely to ascribe absolute value). Popular, too, because of the immediacy of the formal execution. It is even too easy now to recognise these summary popular heroes and perhaps politicise them after reading so much writing on the heroes of our times. But, in Italy, in 1929 they could have faced the little men of Rosai with a yes or no, as they indulged their taste for obscure elegies on some village scene, and they would have got no comfort from them. Even as early as 1929–at his very start–Marini was the only man in Italy, possibly the only artist anywhere, truly popular, through his ability to touch universal themes and re-fashion them into myth which was itself universal.

Ersilia

Pls. 22, 23, Fig. 3

Let us now consider the outstanding examples of works which continue the thought cycle and expound the kind of archetypal theory that Marini first expressed in *The People*. His socially archaic myth reaches its peak in 1930–1 with *Ersilia*. From the existing version in wood dating from 1949 it is quite easy to reconstruct the original in terracotta which was lost during the Second World War. To judge from extant photographs, one quality of the earlier work persists in the later: the obscure hint of the urge to encompass a universal type. This may be taken from some early mother such as the one from Chianciano, but so laden is it with contemporary significance that, even more than *The People* it cuts short any attempt to specify the exact origins of its form. It is fair to assume that, granted the artist's later, deeper penetration into reality, the wood figure of 1949 has a much maturer ethical consistency, and its own realisation in terms of form suggest a space that is the less harshly manipulated as it is the more deliberately and strictly defined. But it is more important to notice that a subject from the 1930s has even twenty years later retained its power to stimulate Marini again–in similar if more evolved terms–to a judgment of reality. And this seems to constitute a kind of historical proof of the inner validity of his attitude towards being. *Ersilia* may indeed be something more than 'a *demoiselle d'Avignon* from the poor district of some provincial Tuscan town' (Carandente).

It is the theme of woman stripped of all inessentials, a concentration of power, deaf defiance and absolute convictions; a myth, in short, that eschews all idealisation. We see in *Ersilia* a total fusion of love-hates, and the choice of total reality in preference to individual, specific definitions of it.

But between *The People* and *Ersilia*, in 1929 and 1930 other works consolidate the impression created in these works, above all *La Borghese* and also the fascinating little idol or *Small Nude* (1929). Then come a *Bather*, *Seated Girl*, *Portrait of Magnelli* and *Self Portrait*. The subject matter of *La Borghese* is complementary to that of *The People*; at the same time it perhaps reveals a critical statement, a basically negative, as opposed to the positive, attitude of the earlier work (Marini is a sculptor of positive realities).

As for the *Small Idol*, if I may substitute a metaphorical name for the real

3 Marxian, I mean, not Marxist. A philosophical, not political, connotation.

Pl. 1

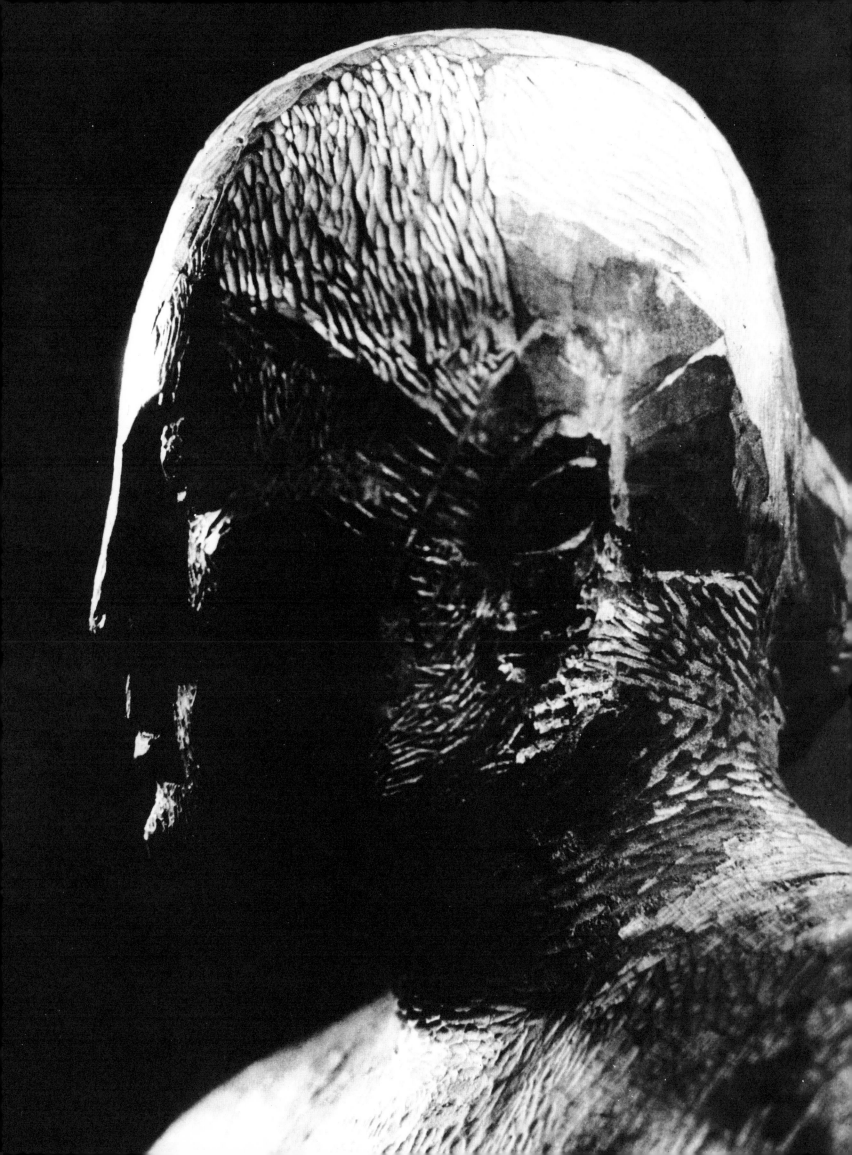

one, the *Small Nude*, how perfect is the amphora-like shape of its thighs, elongated till the torso seems cast from an ancient mould. How lovely too are the suggestion of primitive red on the stomach and round the breast, and the rough sweetness of the black lines on the pubis. Such perfection invites us to discard the language of criticism and take to that of literature. In fact this goddess, newly emerged like a fragile potsherd from the excavations of an enamoured archaeologist, could be the Aegis of a new Parthenia, like the one written by the Greek lyric poet Alcman ('Now I sing of the light of Aegis'). In fact it probably represents Marini's earliest acceptance of a beauty deliberately intended to be eternal and normative, and therefore immersed in the mythical, timeless atmosphere of antiquity. (Two years earlier the *Girl from Algiers*, oil on wood, still contained traces of episodic or realistic sensuality such as typify the Roman School, as Russoli has pointed out.)

Still, even at this early date, Marini's position in relation to reality, is already clearly delineated and has achieved absolute results, such as *Ersilia*, Pl. 2 and in the Goldman bas-relief. This shows an extreme formal simplification of figures against a scarred background. On the right are a horse and rider which appear hardly more than a geometrical sketch though this in turn is contradicted by the way the light plays over it. The meaning of this group of men—or beings—in a space which is both suspended and full of vital movement, can only be understood by referring to Marini's original search for a presence which is significant by the mere fact of its existence.

To form a considered opinion we must take note of the polemical undertone of this intuition and relate it to contemporary experience, both in politics (consider the theoretical constructions by which politicians were trying to change the basic values of existence in Italy at that time) and language (and probably the only realism dialectically valid in relation to non-figurative art in Italy was that of Marini).[4]

The Bamberg Riders

The third archetypal premise and absolute achievement is the *Rider*, of 1936, in the Jesi collection. Marini himself recalls its source 'On my travels through Italy, I was never impressed by the equestrian monuments of Rome, Venice or Padua, but, the one in Bamberg, Germany, made a tremendous impact, perhaps because it came to light in a fairy-tale world, far away from Pl. 3 us, in a forgotten corner. . . .'[5] The Jesi *Rider* was born in fact two years after the German journey. Marini's reference to Rome, Venice and Padua obviously infers the Capitoline *Marcus Aurelius*, the *Colleoni* by Verrocchio and Donatello's *Gattamelata*. These works, as suggested above, demonstrate a historical sequence, a critical not intuitive, temporal not timeless, connection. Bamberg, on the other hand, with its myth-riders ('in a fairy-tale world . . . in a forgotten corner . . .') is another embodiment of a suddenly evoked reality, the occasion for defining once again, like the Etruscans, the incontestable presence of being.

However, there is no direct cultural reference. If the Jesi *Rider* reveals traces of Gothic angularity it is soon to be transformed into Mediterranean fullness in the *Man on Horseback* of 1937 and beyond all doubt in the extra- Pls. 4, 5 ordinary *Horse* of 1939. Yet the centaur motif was present in Marini's consciousness as we have seen from the time of the Goldman bas-relief. Bamberg then must have been a similar impetus, the purely emotional confirmation of a thought that was already itself concrete. Certain other facts need be recalled, I think, at this point. One of these is T'ang ceramics, another, from his life, the flight of some citizens on horseback which stayed in the sculptor's memory as a wonderfully evocative manifestation of form-in-substance. The reference to T'ang involves an emphasis on style, a formal comparison which is much too simple and therefore vain. The flight of those people from their land, driven by terror to an utterly primitive reaction

4 Beyond that of Morandi, which is diametrically opposed as well as abstract. As for the movement that actually took its name from it, I do not consider it relevant even to discuss it here.
5 In M. Venturoli, 'The Sculptor Marino Marini in Italy and Europe', *Le Ore*, 10th February 1966.

4. *Small Boxer*
1935, bronze
base $3\frac{1}{2} \times 5\frac{1}{4}$ in (8×13 cm)
height $8\frac{1}{2}$ in (21 cm)
A. Westholme collection,
Göteborg

(the event took place during the war) is certainly more pregnant with possibilities. It is also narrative; and this goes one further step towards showing the consistently concrete character of Marini's feeling.

If—remembering Bamberg—we are now ready to embark on a discussion of form based upon our interpretation of surfaces we are bound to comment that the Gothic experience is immediately fused with the constant sources of Marini's inspiration. In the *Pilgrim* of 1939 we see a plausible count, whose   Pl. 6 forefathers were probably crusaders, wearing no breastplate, but armoured naturally in the planed curve of his chest and legs. Above the body rises a suffering 'Etruscan' face, its forehead fretted with lines, and with penetrating eyes. But unless we take this merely as an amusing exercise in classification which looks no further than itself, such analysis is a waste of time. At best it serves only to show how Marini is already well able to play with mixed cards in his subtle game of form, in which the ancient myth of *The People* and *Ersilia* is renewed with heightened significance. Far better to point out that by taking up an eternal reality of being, again non-historical, namely that of the Middle Ages, and aligning it with that of antiquity, Marini shows his need to identify himself with an absolute which he understands to be constant, and which presents itself as a definitive image of being in the totality of its presence. It is from this absolute that the ideas draw their meaning, just as the *Pomonas* draw theirs from their connection with antiquity. Both are characters that could disappear behind the charm of their surfaces, if they were understood only in their narrative instead of their mythical, symbolic sense.

Their medieval and ancient connection goes beyond the simple datum of memory. From the very beginning Marini has constantly employed a language of strict compositional logic which is perfectly balanced and finds its own enrichment within itself. We may certainly agree, but only to a limited extent, with Brandi's comment 'It is clear to anyone who is not content with first impressions, that the range of images does not simply start with Maillol and end with T'ang. Nor, if these names may be legiti-

5. *Horse*
1939, bronze
height 46½ in (118 cm)
length 61¼ in (155 cm)
Jesi collection,
Milan

6. *Small Nude*
1943, bronze
height 12¾ in (32 cm)
Property of the artist,
Milan

mately used at all, are they applied to the earlier rather than later inspiration of his figures. It is true that the plastic theme, endlessly varied by the artist, begins there and goes full circle to conclude there: at the same time it fuses the form within that circle.'[6]

It is not in my view so much a plastic theme that is interpreted in various ways as a sentimental, mythical one, though it may well contain a suggestion of form that is immediately transcribed by Marini into his own essential language.

On the other hand, Brandi outlines the difficulty when he states, just before the other comments we quoted: 'to say that there is always a formal problem at the base of Marini's art, which we would not deny,[7] does not suffice to explain his sculpture. It does not suffice because nowadays a premise like this, if isolated from the particular historical context of a consciousness which seeks and chooses for itself, might easily be applied to abstract re-search into form. According to this argument, once set along the road to simplification and condensation of mass, Marini's sculpture ought to have gone even further than it did, to the creation of cubes, spheres and cylinders. The artist does not, however, progress from the object to its geometric element, but takes – if anything – the opposite course.'

6 C. Brandi. From 'Voyage of discovery in modern sculpture: Marino Marini', in *L'Immagine*, II, 16, 1951.
7 But which we do not entirely accept. A 'formal problem' is possibly no more than a formula, a pretext for justifying the interpretation of the linguistic terms to which the critic especially draws attention. In fact I consider that what lies at the root of Marini's sculpture, as of every artistic activity, is a problem of content, in a specific, not generic, sense: 'what I have to say and how I say it'. Too often, in my view, 'how' is substituted for 'what'.

Simplicity and universality of the concept of existence

But what doubts–or anxieties–interrupt the course of horses and Pomonas with the *Miracle* in 1943? Up until then the form had expanded into supreme fullness. We have already mentioned the *Horse* of 1939; we should also cite –to complete the list–the *Pomona* of 1941, perhaps the taller of the two *Young Girls* of 1938 and 1939, the *Pomona* and *Composition* of 1940, the *Naked Venus* and the *Bather* of 1942. The subject of woman, as it is developed from *Ersilia* to the *Small Idol*, is stripped of all clothing as of every contingent accessory. It becomes total presence whose constant existence in our reality cannot be explained in words without recourse to formalistic evasions. The solid volumes concentrate the light on the masterly beauty of their scarred, coloured and marked surfaces. Spatial limits are created and defined by the geometric harmony of their gently turning profiles.

In reality these images translate our own deep sense of existence into significant forms. These are the perpetual symbols of being, which define a substance and concept so simple, because so radical and universal, that we can hardly apply words to them, as they cannot be analysed or synthesised. With these works the first period ends; one whose whole course is at first sight so unified and stylistically constant (we have seen how the *Ersilias* of 1930 and 1949 could come from the same period) as to suggest quite deceptively that a *Horse* of 1939 and one of 1948 are contemporary or a *Pomona* of 1941 and a *Dancer* of 1949. So much so that the *Miracle* of 1943, mentioned above, together with the other two works that are most closely associated with it, the two *Archangels* of the same year, might seem 'a transitory moment in the sculptor's activity when a shadow seems to have passed fleetingly over the luminosity of his forms' (Carandente).[8] Furthermore, even after a simple interpretation without touching the profound spiritual change to which these plasters bear witness, it is hard to believe that a denial of their existence would not ultimately have some meaning for some of the later works expressing affliction. This is especially true for the angular drama of some of his last sculptures, like the two *Warriors* of 1959–66 and 1967, or the *Form of an Idea* of 1966. Not to mention, of course, the psychological import that was transmitted into some of the most deeply-felt portraits, like the *Chagall* of 1962.

In fact the course of Marini's work up until the war shows extreme continuity of thought. We have already stated that it is constantly concerned with positive realities, and–right at the beginning, to clarify the idea of myth in his work–that it is the affirmation of all that may be saved in the universe *vis-à-vis* the fragile or negative aspects of contingency. All of this is true until the year 1942. If, later, the attitude does not exactly change, it grows richer with the record of pain, as for example, in his *Miracle*, which may strike us as an expression of affliction but does not abandon the dialogue with light. This dialogue is sometimes even crudely suggestive, as is the use of colour, which after the superb archaeological evocation of the *Small Idol* reddens like a wound, and eventually becomes almost more than real (see for example the *Small Rider* of 1949).

Pl. 25

Let us now, then, summarise his activity before, and up to 1942 as Marino does, we may claim, by bringing an end to his archaeological phase with the *Quadriga* in the Kunstmuseum in Basel. The *Quadriga* is the reworking of a metope from the Heraeum at the gates of Sele, near Paestum, which shows the sun's chariot. So it is not the manifestation of a recurrent idea of the eternal which is reproduced in a succession of works, such as the urns and canopies, but an exact, definable subject on which to sound the truths of his earlier discoveries with greater subtlety. Once again myth shows its adaptability to modern thought in the impassable presence of the horses, among

Pl. 8

7. *The Archangel* 1943, coloured plaster height 51¼ in (130 cm) Bernouilli collection, Basel

8. *The Archangel* (detail)

---

8 Elsewhere, Carandente himself has well understood the meaning and quality of the *Miracle*: 'The vertical emphasis of this and the other plasters, the wasted simplicity of their forms, the absence of irony, the painful dignity which is rigidly contained in their character, their bewildered melancholy all give them the air of grieving witnesses of history. In its pained composition, in its humble poverty and degradation, in its opacity, and in the meanness of its material, this *Miracle* does not disperse into space, or interact with light but creates a kind of diaphragm between its plastic consistency and the womb of atmosphere in which it is enclosed' (G. Carandente *op. cit.*).

9. *Small Pomona*
1944, bronze
height 19 in (48 cm)
base 3 × 5¾ in (8 × 15 cm)
Property of the artist,
Milan

10. *Portrait of Carlo Carrà*
1944, lead
height 9¼ in (24 cm)
Jesi collection,
Milan

which there just appears–but with what urgency–the figure of the sun-man (perhaps it is Phaeton on the verge of his plunge from myth to destruc-tion, after burning the earth and its crops).

Thus, in these years of his early maturity, Marini reveals the full range of his formal activity. The aggressive adoption of themes from antiquity, which appeared almost instantaneously modernised in *The People*, turns in the *Quadriga* thirteen years later, into a deliberate figurative assessment of his own culture: a judgment of reality. It is a certain fact that the two works stand at opposite ends of a most consistent range of activity. Yet some pieces, like the *Sketch for a Boxer* of 1935 (Jane Wade collection) and the *Boxer* itself (Westholme collection) intervene and raise doubts whether the fullness of forms is not breaking up into more questioning surfaces; while their mass acquires the suggestion of something desperate (a mass that is here more Gothic than in any of the *Riders*).

Fig. 4

Marini's doubts are evinced by certain portraits, also produced in 1942. *Arturo Tosi, Campigli, Paolo Pedrazzini,* and especially the one, a year older, of *De Pisis*. Here the conquest of form won in the previous decade or fifteen years is exercised in an insistent psychological enquiry which strikes us as the agonised search for the individual amid the reality he affirms.

**The
psychological articulation
of the portrait.
The theme of
the Miracle**

Thus, in these heads the thought that gave birth to the *Miracle* may be found, granted that they demonstrate a gradual process of individualisation, which is the new Marinian theme. His attempt to grasp being is modified; he abandons the types he assumed for a total expression of reality for individual ones which may be called anguished manifestations of this reality.

Marini's own words are all the more significant on this subject: 'I am presented with a shape, a profile: and the first thing is the type of this shape, whether round or elongated. These are essential elements; you must first

12. *Pomona*
1945, stone
height 69 in (175 cm)
Werner and Nelly Bär collection,
Zürich

13. *Seated Pomona*
1946, bronze
height 17¼ in (44 cm)
Jesi collection,
Milan

22

find them out then fix them in your mind. After this I try to get inside the spirit of the character and here there is great difficulty in imagining this physiognomy on the scale of humanity; that is, what it represents to other men, other human personalities. When I've done that it's finished. This truth has to persist inside me until I have completed the portrait. The result must also satisfy me in vitality of expression and the realisation of the true typical features of the sitter. When this obligation is fulfilled, when the subject is now transferred to the realm of the dead who are alive forever, I hand over the work to my client–who, unfortunately, is hardly ever pleased, but *tant pis.*'[9] If we want to analyse this testament of faith we must emphasise two points: first, the 'figurative' capability of the image ('the quality of this shape–whether round or elongated'): second, and decisively, the need to find a connection between a universal intuition ('the scale of humanity') and the individual which is, as he says, the particular manifestation of this universality which has to be transformed again into a fresh universal symbol.

Pl. 9   But to return to the *Miracle*. The title surely goes beyond the shape, which is that of a suffering man, whose worn bone of a head lolls on the sharp angle of his wasted shoulders. We might say that it is not so much a miracle in being, the revelation of a deity, as the expectation of such a revelation. The symbol in the individual (whose face has the pathos of a portrait) is that of a humanity stripped of all certainty, standing in front of a void which the divinity ought to fill. God–some people believe–needs man: only in this grieving specimen of humanity can transcendence have meaning, when God takes on human form and receives the miracle of existence from man.

If this is true–how can we doubt that this Gothic, expressionistic moment is an essential stage, and a determining one, in the course of Marini's development? It is here that critical analysis itself, like Marini, needs eternal symbols so that definitions which are in themselves historical, may effectively stand outside history. I cannot overemphasise the Gothic style of the *Miracle*. But this may be generally agreed only if it is understood in the sense of a

9 'Marino Marini als Portratist', *Du*, October 1963.

24

relation between composition and mass which permits disquieting allusions to appear. The man of the *Miracle*, then, is open to the vibrations of its composition while the mass of the *Horse* of 1939 or the *Pomona* of 1941 is closed.

However, we ought just to note that the portraits of 1942 and some even earlier experiments were already signposts along this road. In 1943 the enchanting small head of his wife – Marina – seems to borrow an Ionic sensitivity from the antique perfection of the *Small Idol*. (We have already cited the *Sketch for a Boxer*, but we might also consider the *Man on Horseback* of 1937.) However, Gothic or not, the true significance of the *Miracle* lies in the acknowledgment of a changed reality, or rather of a spiritual, perceptual change in Marini from what we might call 'atonal', great definitions, to perceptions of the individual as a symbol.

This meaning is immediately to be found in the two other plasters associated with the *Miracle*, the two *Archangels* (we might call them a triptych). In a series of metopes, however, (the *Three Graces*, *Small Rider*, *Composition*) and in some small *Pomonas*, all dating from 1943, the plastic object permits light to play over it in an experiment which is in some way naturalistic and therefore apparently different from the recognition of transcendence which characterises the plasters. In fact they can be similarly interpreted. When he lost the certainty with which he had earlier expounded the total positivity of being, in the compact volume of simple heroes, Marino embarked on a new dialogue, in the critical year of 1942. In this dialogue between divinity, nature and man, man polarises the essential significance of divinity and nature within each other. We may even say that a new man is born from it, like the *Juggler* and *Dancer* of 1944, and that the argument is pursued much further in the riders and warriors that were to come.

Divinity, nature and man
Figs. 7, 8

Pl. 10

It is in these terms that we should see the Cohen *Small Rider* of 1944. The root feeling has not only remained, but seems to have reverted to the primitive violence of his youthful works. In his choice of form he reveals the need for an entirely natural basis of existence, expressed now with a completely new intensity. He rejects every culture as a damaging formalisation and defends a value that is not only single, but the very essence of being. Thus the horse turns into a little bull and the man a powerful, wounded piece of matter which carries with it the marks of an inadvised, cruel tragedy. The *Small Rider* possibly reveals the most poignant and painful moment in Marino's crisis, a record of which he could not help making. But the same is true of the contemporary *Juggler*. In this the brutal weight of the torso, so weary on the fragile, bent and webbed legs, rises to a point at which the head is turned away, recalling the *Boxer* of 1935. This is an image of disinheritance, a fragment of humanity impersonating humanity, a suppliant to heaven. Even more exhausting are the weight and feeling of the matter in the *Dancer*, in which the pitiless misery of the three small *Pomonas* of the preceding year reaches its highest implication.

Pl. 12

Immediately afterwards, he seems to have gone back to the poetic intuition which he had abandoned in the years before 1939 (and which he had also expressed in 1943 with his latest masterpiece, the *Young Girl*, in the Nelly Bär collection). This is especially evident in the great *Judith*, in Antwerp Museum, and in other big nudes, dancing Venuses and Pomonas. In reality these works betray a pause, a slackening in the tension that had so vehemently upset Marino's formal and spiritual certainty in 1943–4. Perhaps it was due to universal relief at the end of the war, the alacrity with which life was resumed, the belief that faith in the simplicity and grandeur of human values was renewable. Thus these works display a kind of brief mannerism or neoclassicism in the sense of a rethinking of his themes, or rather of his 'classical' forms. However, that is true only to a certain extent, granted that the effective enrichment of the preceding period did not fail to give these works too a relation with nature. (Their volumes expand in a more articulated

**The 'neo-classicism'
of 1945**
Pl. 11

space, they have a more laborious weight.) This derives directly from the nudes of 1944, while some portraits, on the other hand (of a *Lady*, or *Fiorenza*, of *Doctor Gasser*, of *Baron von Schumacher*, of *Mme Grandjean* and especially of *Georg Schmidt*) are clearly related thematically with the two *Archangels*.

This moment cannot be understood in isolation, the pause was really composed out of the two preceding phases. It was necessary, too, to the work that Marino felt he must prepare to accomplish, the laborious reconstruction of man. From this replay of all the cards of his doubts and convictions, there at last came to light in 1946, like a knowing Eve, the small *Seated Pomona*. In this Marini seems to have by-passed all his myths and gone back to earliest antiquity and to have tried to rediscover a truth even prior to that of the Etruscans or the Greeks in a prehistoric Venus, in *Laussel* or the *Red Leaps*. This allusion to a past epoch, although hypothetical, is not without significance, since it enables one to find the spirit of Marini at that moment; just as, via the Etruscan or medieval myth, one was able to discover an earlier judgment of reality. Here Marini is more than ever face-to-face with the roots of being, but while he finds nothing to hand–a single quantity on which to count–except the weight of life, he denies, through the deepest convictions of his spirit, that it can only be material. He also reconstructs his sense of history, one might say, *ab imis fundamentis*, and rediscovers his perpetual matrix. Thus he vindicates as never before the repeated, insistent name of Pomona, who now becomes the absolute symbol of primordial fertility (of feeling, spirit, pain and love): *hominum divomque voluptas*.

From this beginning, or rather resumption, Marino's last, greatest works are born. Once his faith is rediscovered, the juggler-beggar becomes the juggler-crucified (or hanged) of 1946: an elongated lozenge of mass from the body thrusts forth in a form of the purest classicism. The type in which Marino had tried to compress the essence of being, suffering the agony of the individual, has come back, after being submerged in the primordial mud of creation, to define a last human myth. Now everything will be possible; the image is apt to express the great themes of pain and love since it has finally attained to being. This had to be preceded by the pure naïvety of *The People*, the magic of Bamberg, the tamed savagery of *Ersilia*, and the astonishment of the *Miracle*. The searcher after relics in 1944 and the refined mannerist of 1945 all had to come first to complete the laboured development–apparently so straightforward–of Marini the man.

Rediscovery of the roots of existence

At this point, then, in 1946, let us resume the thread of our discussion of the main episodes in his work. Once he rediscovered his initial certainty, Marini was able to bring to fruition all his vital, earlier experiments. In the *Small Rider* from the Modern Art Museum in Kyoto, the 'presence' of Pomona-Eve-Venus merges with the ancient myth of the centaur. At the same time it is enriched with emotional understanding of the individual, colour and light playing a decisive role in this analysis of the agony of existence. (Its surfaces are repeatedly scratched and gouged, gashed, almost enflamed by brilliant reds and leaden purplish-blues.) On the other hand, the earliest balance of volume, already so painfully called into question by its relation to local circumstances, is now flattened out into the crossing of two lines; one is that of the horse, the other, stretched in a spasm of adhesion and permanence in being, of the rider. This crossing of lines becomes the stamp, increasingly simplified and meaningful, of the similar compositions still to come (and reaches its sharpest point of tension in the new realisations of the *Miracle* theme).

Referring backwards from this *Rider* to the *Seated Pomona*, the Cohen *Rider* and the *Juggler* of 1944, we may be assailed by doubts whether Marini produced anything but a series of monsters out of the ruins of war. With his canons of beauty smashed–the beauty that is still witnessed in the *Young Girl* of 1943 and reaffirmed above all in the big marbles of 1945–we might begin to think that Marini's divine optimism is waning. His faith in a

Fig. 13

Pl. 15

Pl. 16

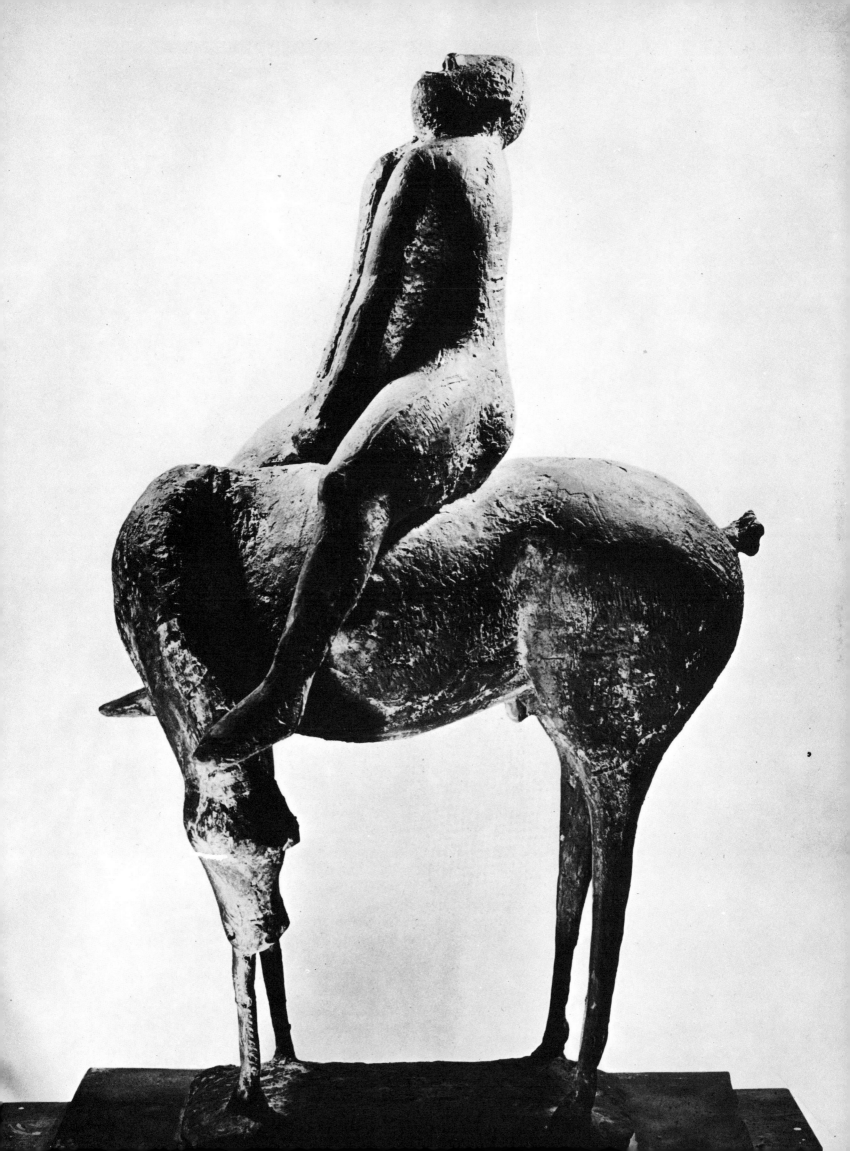

16. *Small Nude* (detail)
1949, bronze
height 19¼ in (49 cm)
R. Jucker collection,
Milan

positive reality manifested to him in the form of myth, now seems to be giving way to the codification of fear, in a sort of reversion to the horse-riders of the apocalypse. This would result in the resurgence of the other side of humanity, the side Marini had stubbornly rejected and defined as only accidental, against which his myths stood out as the choice of the absolute, as a counter proposition with eternal claims. Such doubt is a simple temptation, above all because it can so easily be fitted into a pattern. Simple, too, because of the hope it gives us to moralise over Marini's last twenty years, to see them as denunciation, and thence as a practical intervention into reality. But such an interpretation would completely disregard or contradict the actual substance of Marini's art. In fact, until the year 1946, Marini had appeared too moved an interpreter of the great human values, progressing from a comprehensive, incontestable affirmation, such as

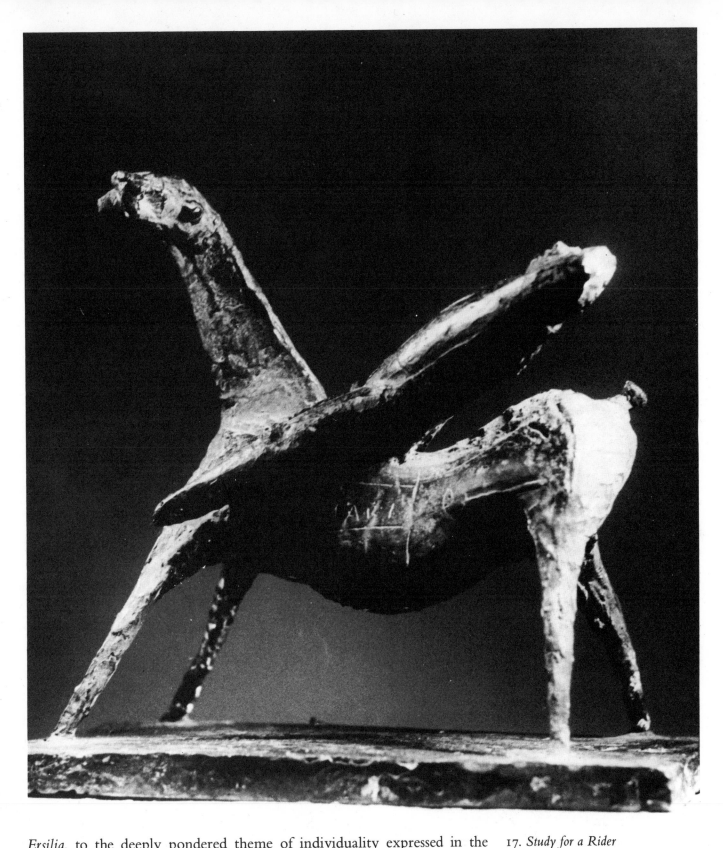

Ersilia, to the deeply pondered theme of individuality expressed in the *Miracle*. He could not suddenly toss this suffering, long-sought world of values back into a melting pot from which new molochs might arise. If these works are monsters, they are monsters that have profoundly explored not only the essential root of what exists *(Seated Pomona)*, but also pain and violence *(Juggler)*. They have been modified in relation to the earlier beauty precisely to the extent that pain, fear and even violence may permit a new, deeper awareness of a positive reality, which bears their wounds and scars.

The apparent ferocity, then, that contorts both the *Juggler* of 1944 and the *Rider* of 1947 (Campilli collection) must be interpreted as the capacity for good in the midst of evil (positive being amid not-being) which needs every one of its existential implications if it is to survive. It needs to be that fertile

17. *Study for a Rider*
1951, bronze
base $7\frac{1}{2} \times 11\frac{3}{4}$ in (19 × 30 cm)
height $10\frac{1}{4}$ in (26 cm)
Heyward Cutting collection,
Chicago

**The theme of pain
and the reconstitution
of man**

slime from which the *Seated Pomona* came, in order to express the spiritual certainty that had suffered so much in the *Miracle*.[10] At this point we may again ask ourselves our earliest question concerning the ethical validity of an art like Marini's, which sublimates reality, and contrast it with the obligation to intervene more directly into reality itself and contest it.

We have already seen that Marini's position implies a judgment of being and this poses queries of a moral order. But it seems to me that after trying to understand the motives of his development by something more than a purely abstract reading of style alone, this morality is so self-evident as to constitute a true and almost unique term of judgment and evaluation.

In 1947 the deeply-thought classicism of the *Juggler* and of the *Riders* of the previous year recurs. In a new series of *Riders*, *Pomonas* and portraits it establishes itself as the theme of pain, with a more balanced appreciation. We have already discussed the Campilli *Rider*, the fruit of an extreme tension which is shown in the man's upturned head (the theme of the *Boxer* of 1935 and the *Juggler* of 1944). Towards this the stiffened line of the man's body thrusts up and makes a cross with the other horizontal line of the horse's twisted neck as it bends to the ground. This cross-rhythm of movements becomes a constant feature, repeated in an unending, and always significant variety of specimens). In the same context we should mention the large *Rider* in the Stedeljk Museum, Amsterdam, another similar one in the Museum of Modern Art in New York, and one in the Jucker collection in Milan. This list is only by way of example and is certainly far from complete. All of them show experimentation with the tension of volumes. This probably finds its peak in the Campilli *Rider*, while the given naturalistic or realistic motif (that is the correspondence between the delineation of its members – face, hands, legs – at their lowest level and evident reality) becomes more and more summary, just as it had the previous year in the prehistoric clay of the *Seated Pomona*. The awestruck *Rider* in the Grandjean collection presents a very close analogy to it, for it too is laborious in the torpid weight of the body, astride the tapir-horse which extends an elongated muzzle towards the unknown or even infinity.

There is a similar core of tension in the *Pomona* of the Jesi collection (an Amazon dismounted from her horse, or an Eve standing up to impose her fertility upon the hellish paradise which is earth). While in the group of portraits (of *Emilio Jesi*, *Riccardo Jucker*, *Dada Pizzocaro*, *Mrs Jecker* and *James Dunn*) there is the same summary handling of features, which gave the *Riders* and *Pomonas* such mask-like faces, whose primordial expressions strive to define the terrible simplicity of their presence. But in them, this corresponds, and not by contradiction, to an increasingly emphatic psychological definition since the reason for the portrait lies in this excavation, in rediscovering the root of feeling and making it an affirmation of being once more.

The history of these shapes and the feelings to which they give expression could be – even now – the current history of Marini. (It would not be neces-

18. *Small Rider* (detail)
1951–2, bronze
base $15\frac{3}{4} \times 9$ in (40×24 cm)
height $22\frac{3}{4}$ in (58 cm)
Bridgestone Museum,
Tokyo

Pl. 17

Pl. 19

Pl. 18

Fig. 14

The second Miracle

---

10 If a quotation from D'Annunzio is the furthest remove from Marinian ideas that one could imagine (not even the most distant relationship exists between the Centaur of the *Death of the Stag* – 'Pointed with two arms, man to below the waist, the rest a stallion with gross genitals' – and a horse and rider, however bestialised, such as that of Cohen) some verses, all the same, spring into my mind from the *Laus Vitae*:

> Then climbed we up
> The rotten wood stair and crossed
> The secret threshold: there perceived
> Pirgo's woman in the shadow
> Of her bed; short and plump,
> Like an expectant she-goat
> With many udders
> Smelling of the ram, her spouse

with all that follows and the limpid promise of the last line:

> Oh how sweet,
> From the harlot's door
> To gaze upon the virgin stars.

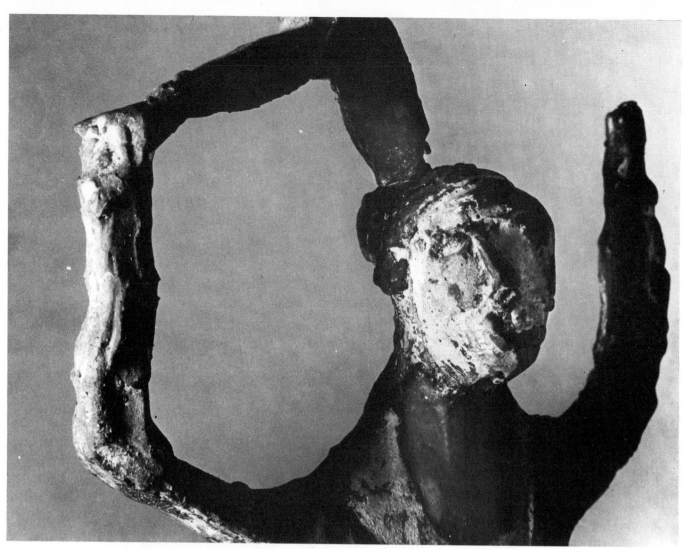

19. On the preceding pages:
The Jugglers (detail)
1953, coloured bronze
height 18 in (46 cm)
Pierre Matisse Gallery,
New York

20. *Small Juggler* (detail)
1953, coloured bronze
height 18½ in (47 cm)
Private collection,
London

sary even to pursue this argument in word, but enough to let the photo-graphs act as interpreters,[11] since photography is also a critical activity and one of the subtlest in its ability to find, in a suitable angle or a relevant play of light, the true meaning of the image.) But in 1953–4 there suddenly emerged the doubt of 'a complete change of direction, in a dramatic sense, of his search for form' (Carandente). To those who think that the *Miracle* of 1943 is a crucial work it will not seem unimportant that this change of direc-tion is signalled by another *Miracle* in 1953–4. Moreover, this was erected (in one of its three bronze castings) by the artist in the square of Rotterdam in memory of the martyrs to freedom. I tend to think that we should view this work and those that follow it not so much as a complete change of direction as the logical development and enlargement of the query that we have been trying to clarify throughout the development of Marini's earlier work. So that it is possibly saying both too much and too little to declare that this is the 'most Gothic and expressionistic of all the artist's works'.

Certainly the Rotterdam *Miracle* is enriched, compared with the one of 1943, by a maturer intensity of expression and mastery of form, but both of them go well beyond the intensifying of a problem of style, such as may be defined by the term Gothic (in its non-historical sense). They also go beyond the admissible limits of feelings which might be defined as 'expressionistic'. Both of them, in short, represent an exact pronouncement about reality: the later work is unthinkable without the arc of experience that separates it from the earlier (or rather, unites it with it). This in turn amounts to the dramatisation of the great themes of myth through the newly-discovered

11 It is probably because of the photographs that Marini in this book appears more dramatic than usual, even in other famous reproductions we have seen. Thus the reader may judge how truthfully the photographer Liberto Perugi has understood Marini's work. As for the present writer, he can do no more than announce that the photographs of Perugi have been of even greater value and assistance to him in the understanding of Marini's sculpture than he can express.

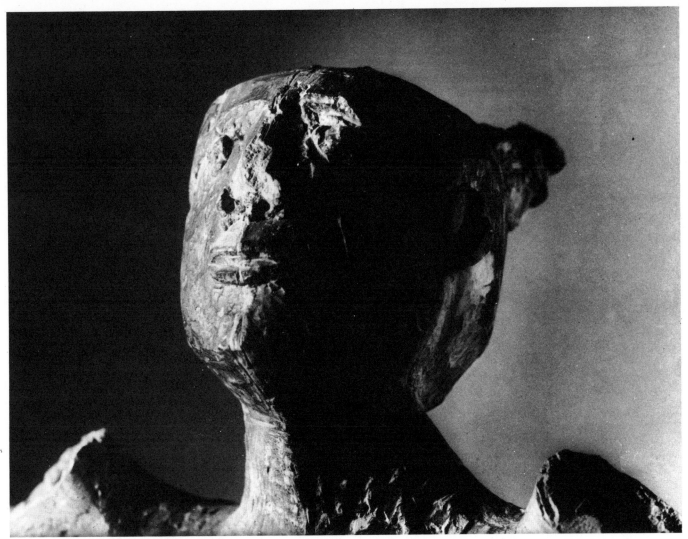

21. *Dancer* (detail)
1953, bronze
height 70 in (178 cm)
H. Krayenbühl collection,
Zürich

symbolism of the individual. Finally he abolishes and reconstructs his language, to arrive at a better-articulated, more profound affirmation of being. (Carandente, writing about the second *Miracle*, offers us an excellent definition of this language; 'The final shape of this plastic motif (no longer the spirited horse standing upright, but both figures, horse and rider, prostrate) has some exceptionally interesting points. There is, in fact, a correspondence between the spread of plastic masses in space and the audacious asymmetry of the relation between voids and substances. At the same time, the irregularity of the projections of volume into the ideal measurements of space creates an endless antinomy between the staticity of the double fall and the dynamism impressed on the whole sculptural block'.[12])

We have seen the various events in this arc as far as 1947. To arrive in sequence at the second *Miracle* we should also mention the Hirshhorn *Rider* of 1949 (the form more summary than ever before – it is the final stage of the Cohen *Rider* – and repeatedly gashed with lacerations of colours), the other from the Kraynbühl collection, of 1949–50, and lastly the one of 1952–3, now in the Werner and Nelly Bär collection. But the new and possibly decisive factor in the extraordinary fecundity of Marini's art during this period is his resumption of painting, which dates from 1948. This resulted in a series of paintings which are complementary to the sculpture. They are not only – as Russoli said in a statement quoted by Carandente in full – 'the combination of a poetic world, of imagination, and of choice of symbolic figures and of a way of seeing and judging reality, but are also a continuation of the linguistic composition and search for form, in the sense that they depend upon a vision entirely personal to the sculptor'.[13] I think we may go further and say that the pictures have had

Pl. 25

Pl. 29

Pls. 34, 35, 37, 38

12 G. Carandente *op. cit.*
13 F. Russoli. *Marino Marini, paintings and drawings*, Milan, 1963.

35

22. *Small Miracle*
1955, bronze
$8\frac{1}{4} \times 9\frac{1}{2}$ in (21×24 cm)
Boboustedt collection,
Kungälv, Sweden

such an experimental value in relation to his sculpture that they have enormously enlarged its stylistic potential. A look at the *Imaginary Games* of 1951 (in the Galerie d'Art Moderne in Basel) or the first *Composition in Green* of 1952 (Private collection, Rome) is enough to confirm this view.

Matter in spirit

However that may be, the last fifteen years of Marini's work (so long has passed since the second *Miracle*) is marked by an extreme freedom in his continuous assessment of being. At the same time, too, he insistently verifies his eternal myths, which are now expressed in increasingly polyhedric intimations of the drama that has become his judgment of reality and that was implicit in the far-distant *People* of 1929. While on this subject it may

Pls. 22, 23, Fig. 3

be necessary to devote a word or two to the second *Ersilia* which dates from 1949 and in which the ancient theme of 1930 has persisted with a tenacity that we might consider innate in the character. Yet it has brought itself dramatically alive again by borrowing from the agony which blossomed from the crisis[14] of 1943 as well as from the impassable fertility of its resumption in 1946. Concièrge's girl or *demoiselle d'Avignon*, myth of womanhood or sum of constant sufferings, this early matron ends as a woman in majesty. It is, at the same time, a vast complex of meanings, the highest symbol of our age and Marini's.

As regards the analysis of his most recent works, we are probably too closely involved in their history to employ any argument except one that is either pure autobiography or pure formal description. In this case we run the risk of pronouncing non-existent abstractions and forcing his expression to fit our assumptions. It will be enough, then, to turn to a few outstanding points and try to build a network of judgments which still reflect early influences and are in some way a confirmation of all that has been handled until now. We shall need to talk about the pattern of development, from the theme of the *Warrior* through the second *Miracle*; and about the great

14 I seem to have used this word 'crisis' several times which has – and must have – an entirely positive meaning. Especially, I may be permitted to repeat, with reference to the years 1943–6.

36

theme of the *Warrior* that appears first in the magnificent group of 1959–60 and again in the extraordinary stone of 1967. (The first sketch of these dates from 1956 – *Idea for the Warrior* – and then comes back repeatedly in a series of intermediate versions.)

It is clear that all the elements of Marini's experience are combined in these works in an extremely explicit manner; the total presence of being, the total redemption of pain, the need for an absolute integrity in composition and the aspiration to a supreme architectonic order. There is an interplay of close relationships which binds together the disarmed *Rider* in the Bechtler collection (1956–7) or his greatest version of it in the Bauwlust in The Hague, with the *Composition of Elements* of 1964–5; or the fiery wood *Miracle* of the Kunstmuseum in Basel (1954) with the various versions of *The Cry* (1961–3).

Once again, we may take the portraits as confirmation of the basic humanity of these victors vanquished, whose cry is petrified in great simplicity of form. Its former fullness is modified in the sense that it becomes a pattern of pure stresses into which faces and bodies are transformed in the gigantic rictus of existence. Portraits crowd out during these years in a memorable series. In them psychological analysis is reduced to an import that loses itself deep within the individual. Thus it goes beyond its individual meaning and draws the most universal significance of humanity from it. So that we ought perhaps to invert Marini's words quoted above and conclude that in these faces the whole world of humanity is reflected. In them we encounter the sense of other men, and other human personalities. We see a Stravinsky greater than the man Stravinsky, or a Chagall greater than Chagall.

Let us go back to look at the works one by one. It may be said that the horse, in the Rotterdam *Miracle*, is prostrate rather than furious. We may, however, find a way to describe its evolution more appropriate than the general one about content and judgment, which we have already referred

23. *Warrior*
1959, bronze
$21\frac{1}{2} \times 13\frac{3}{4}$ in (55×35 cm)
Pierre Matisse Gallery,
New York

Figs. 26, 27
Pls. 31, 32

Pl. 28
Pl. 36

**From the Miracle
to the Warrior**

to (and which dates from at least ten years earlier). This evolution dates back to the middle version of the subject (the furious one) from 1951–2 in which the edginess and the relationship between lines and stresses, which he experimented with in his painting, together indicate an extremely savage vision, which denies any softening whatsoever from the material. We can probably say that here Marini rejects once and for all any equivalence of naturalistic character between the articulation of what is and the quality of his expressive medium. In the preceding years (especially before 1946) this had probably influenced his judgment of reality in such a way that he conceived beauty as innate in his material and bursting forth from it.

Pl. 30, Fig. 21

Figs. 19, 20

This is apparent not only in the dancers that followed immediately, born in a direct line from the hanged *Juggler* of 1946, but in the acrobats and jugglers too, from the same period as the Rotterdam *Miracle* ('a crowd of beings tossed about by storms, who have taken refuge on the furthest bank of unreality. The work is on the borders of sarcasm' (Carandente).) Only we must not forget that these figures have lost none of their symbolic significance, and aspire to represent humanity not by means of dancing, however tossed about (which would be substituting Ionesco for Marini), but by preserving its ultimate truth: the doubt in which the survival of a final morality becomes possible.

The subject is worked out in several versions similar to the Rotterdam *Miracle* in which Marino's repetition of the subject pursues an essentiality of image ever more insistent. He defines once and for all the symbols in which he is attempting to enclose the drama of humanity – another proposition of the myth – which has already been identified as the 'total' subject of all his

26. *Composition of Elements*
1964–5, bronze
height 41¼ in (105 cm)
base 112¼ × 53 in (285 × 140 cm)
Property of the artist,
Milan

27. *Composition of Elements*
1965, tempera on paper
53 × 28 in (135 × 70 cm)
Property of the artist,
Milan

works. From this same spiritual condition grows the theme of the warrior in which, therefore, I do not believe it possible to distinguish the metaphor of man becoming a machine of war. It is, much rather, the last defence of the individuality of man as a 'totality' of value (a kind of rider after the miracle) which puts itself forward as a portrait of humanity dug out of its own history. As we said at the start, it is mythical in the sense that it affirms all that may be saved; and is already transformed into spirit, in the dramatic, ever more profound absolution of matter.

The first versions of the *Warrior* date from 1956. The point of arrival and departure is indicated in the group of 1959–60 and is noted in the sculptor's own words incised on the base of the first casting: 'a desolate song has gone out over the world'. These words probably surpass the existential signifi-

40

28. *Portrait of Mies van der Rohe*
1967, bronze
height 13 in (33 cm)
Nationalgalerie, Berlin

cance of the work itself in lyric and elegiac quality. It is not abandonment to the contemplation of pain that finds poetic confirmation in this work, but the construction of man within and not outside the tragedy. Thus we should understand the song of desolation not so much the subject of the *Warrior*, as the objective, so to speak, spiritual state (reality) in which man, tortured and transfixed, rebuilds his own being. (Thus it is art as an intervention into reality, aiming to modify it, implying both judgment and ethical and political attitudes.)

The themes of miracle and warrior give birth to another, the *Composition of Elements* (first version 1960) in which—as if to emphasise the universality of the symbol—not only are the naturalistic and figurative data consumed, but the title is also reduced to the mere record of a scheme.

Figs. 26, 27

There is a schematic interaction between the *Composition of Elements* (which reappears in various versions the following years, both in sculpture and painting) and the group of *The Cry* 1961–2 oil on paper; 1962 and 1963 bronzes). In this the subject of the *Warrior* strives through extreme violation of form towards a symbolism that is possibly the most despairing that Marini has ever expressed. Just as in 1946 the *Seated Pomona* and associated works had signified total conquest of the natural quality of man, so here it seems that Marini is striving to recapture, after the tragedy, the primordial quality of feelings, the re-awakening of the consciousness of existence.

The numerous themes have now come together in a substantial unity.

Pl. 39 In 1966 the extraordinary bronze called *A Form in an Idea* combines the cry of the warrior after the miracle with the drama of the jugglers, acrobats and dancers. This is no caricature of humanity, nor the inverted equilibrium of a world that rotates in absurdity. It is the tragic fixity of the acts necessary to life, the redemption of human dignity in the tragedy of its situations, and, in short, a conclusion not so different—in the intense power of its experience—from the one Marini had reached twenty or thirty years before in *The People* and *Ersilia*.

Pl. 40 So, in his final stage (in which the huge *Warrior* of 1967 is one of his most recent comments and certainly among the largest), he shows once more that his work is still concerned with the perception of a basic human value. This value has been asserted in the myths, at once simple and rich, with *Riders* and *Pomonas*; has survived the emaciating tragedy of the *Miracles*, and has been dug up and brought to its most fundamental significance in the *Warriors*. Agonisingly experienced in the universal psychology of the portraits, the theme of Marini's work has been, and is, man; God or monster, Olympian, or devoured by the flames of a concrete purgatory, aware of his happiness, aware of his agony, but ever toiling over the heavy task of finding his own positive humanity.

In this excavation Marini has built up what we have defined as his myths. Once their range has been reviewed, it is easier perhaps to appreciate the value of the term, apart from each detail of its narrative or fairy-tale growth. Thus it is seen to be the assiduously cherished symbol of present history which is rediscovered in a past understood in terms of eternity.

Beyond every external, casual reference to other cultures, Marini has gone about searching for his own history in the totality and immediacy of its values. These might happen to coincide poetically with Etruscan terracottas or Gothic carvings, or again with prehistoric lava and Greek marbles. But his history, let us repeat, is necessarily contemporary. What exactly is the importance of this meditation to the awareness of his contemporaries is a question that might create a crisis rather than a certainty. But there remains the fact that the monuments (to use a word that belongs to a very different history) in The Hague and Rotterdam indicate a positive relationship between people and artist and broadly verify therefore that positiveness which is at the very root of Marini's work.

Thus we should probably conclude that herein, especially, lies the truth of this witness or rather prophet of our time.[15]

15 Here I end this essay (which I—like others—have used to try to clarify my own ideas on contemporary art by following the development of one of its greatest exponents). I had long wondered whether I should wait for an opportunity to pursue the last ten or fifteen years of Marini's activity in greater detail. I decided not to, chiefly because I seem unable to discover the final 'crisis' of this period, and thus to judge his 'morality' competently. By morality I mean the direction of his intervention into a reality which is obviously itself in a state of agonising change. It certainly would not be difficult to build a vocabulary, as others have done, and are doing (which would result in a kind of pseudo-vocabulary) through a so-called stylistic assessment of his work. But this would have gone against my absolute conviction that this type of enquiry makes no real contribution to history. Basically I believe that an obviously problematical attitude such as Marini's at present, allows us only, or mainly, to examine its make-up which is what I have tried to do. In compiling the book, I have also made use of a bibliography which I have tried to make as complete as possible, as well as the plan for a catalogue which may serve as a point of reference if nothing else. Not to mention, of course, the photographs which are probably its principal merit.

1

2

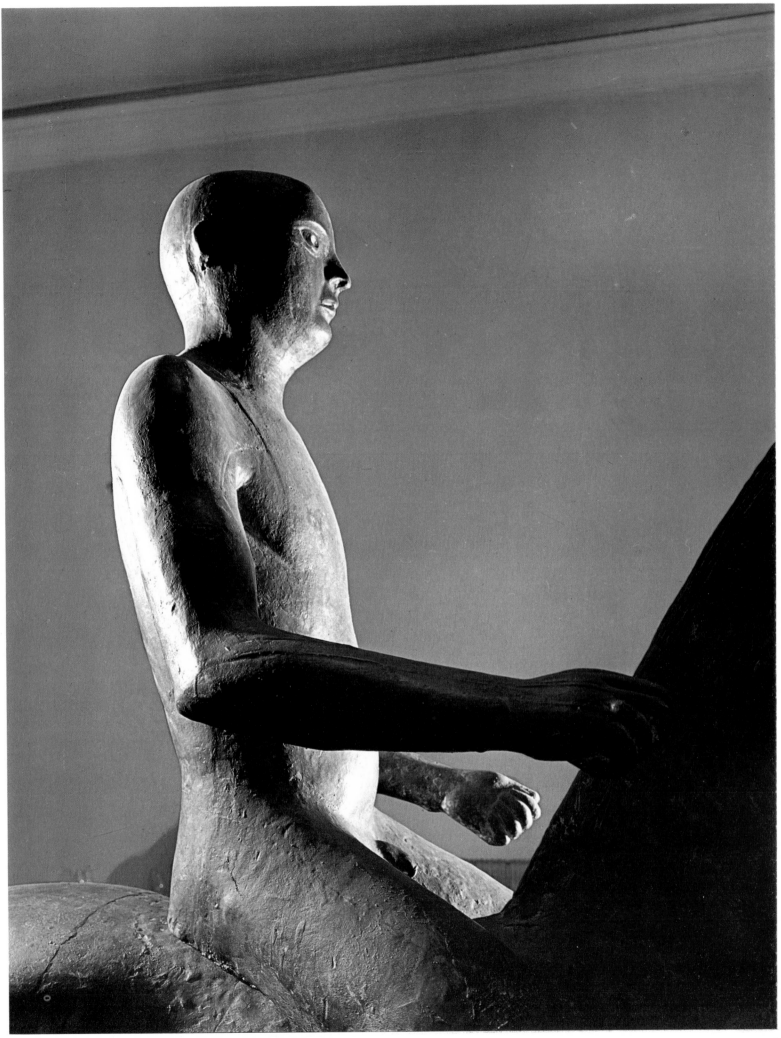

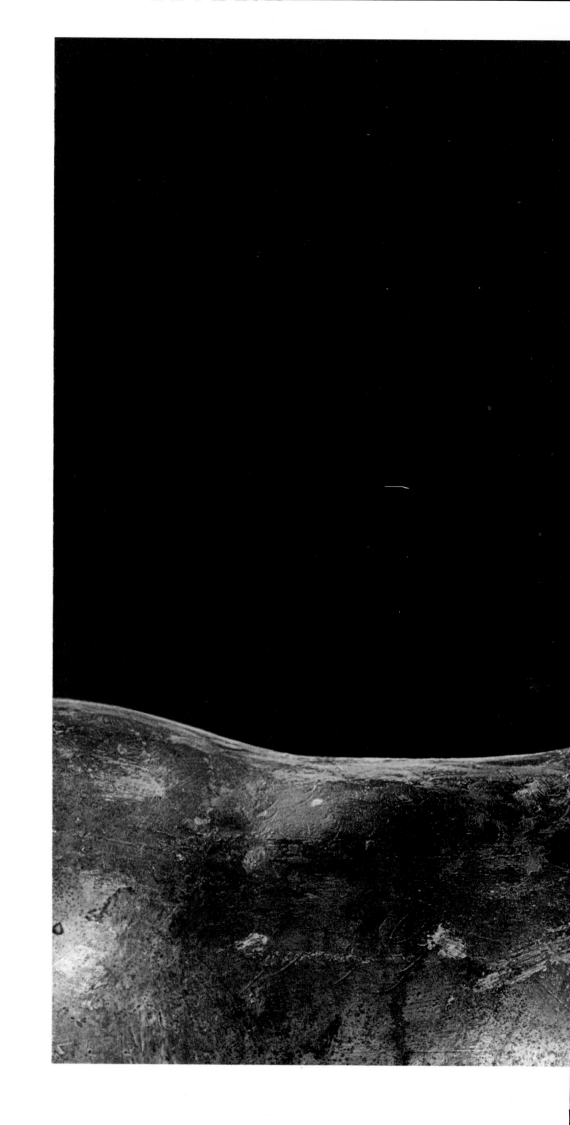

4-5

6

8

12

14

15

16

18

20-21

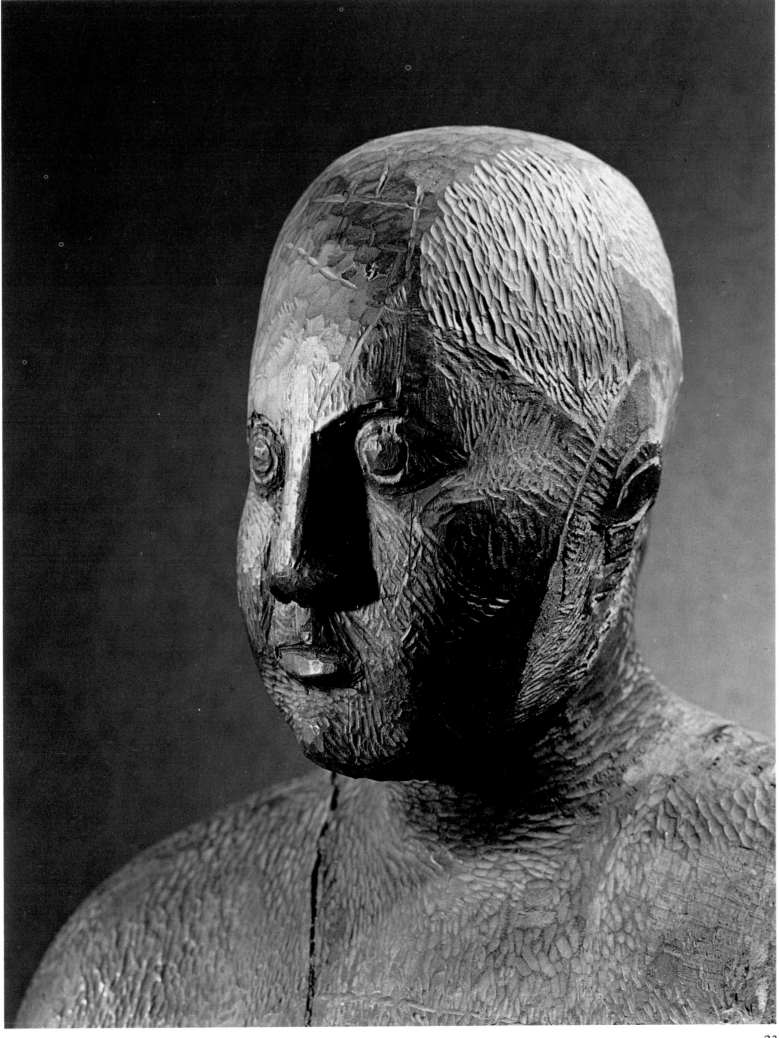

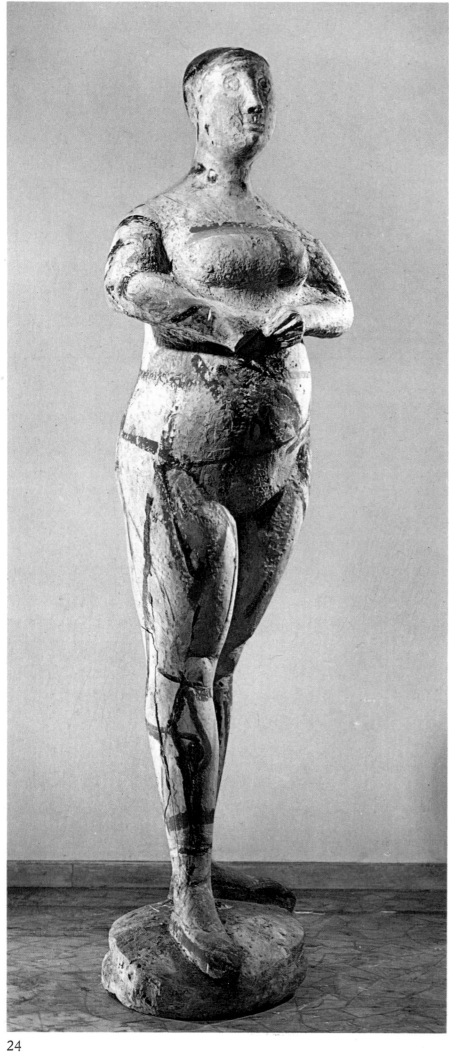

24

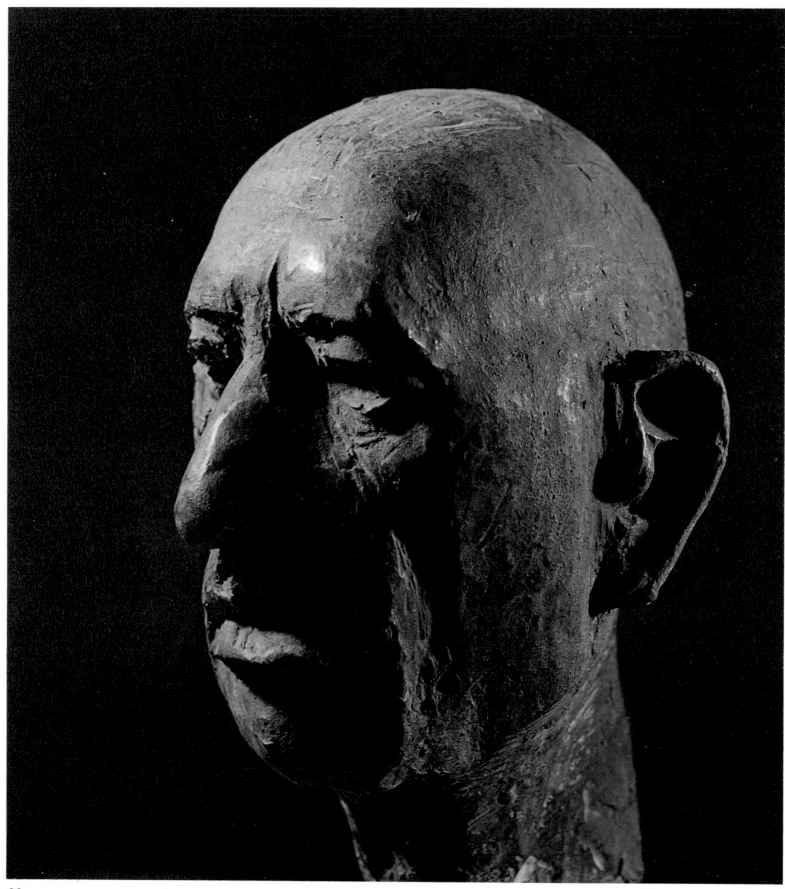

28

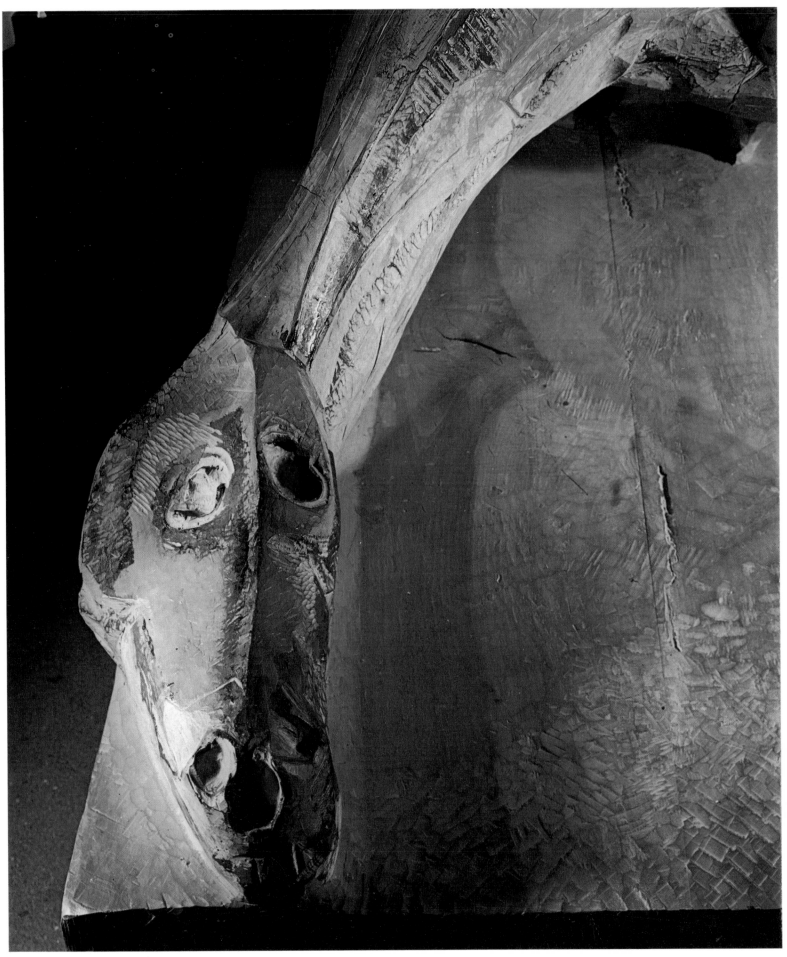

33

34

36

38

40

Description of colour plates

1 *Small Nude*
1929, polychrome plaster, height $8\frac{3}{4}$ in (22 cm)
Marina Marini collection, Milan

2 *Composition*
1932, bronze, $28\frac{1}{2} \times 24\frac{3}{4}$ in (72×63 cm)
Maurice Goldman collection, London

3 *Rider* (detail)
1936, bronze, base 15×53 in (38×135 cm) height $78\frac{3}{4}$ in (200 cm)
Jesi collection, Milan

4–5 *Horse* (detail)
1939, bronze, base $13\frac{1}{2} \times 29$ in (34×74 cm) height $49\frac{1}{4}$ in (125 cm)
Nelly Bär collection, Zürich

6 *The Pilgrim*
1939, bronze, base $16 \times 48\frac{3}{4}$ in (41×124 cm) height 68 in (173 cm)
Jesi collection, Milan

7 *Pomona*
1941, bronze, height 63 in (160 cm)
Musées Royaux des Beaux Arts, Brussels

8 *The Quadriga*
1942, terracotta, $17\frac{3}{4} \times 16\frac{1}{2}$ in (45×42 cm)
Kunstmuseum, Basel

9 *Miracle* (detail)
1943, polychrome plaster, height $27\frac{1}{2}$ in (70 cm)
Jesi collection, Milan

10 *Three small Pomonas*
1943, bronze, height $16\frac{1}{2}$ in (43 cm)
Marina Marini collection, Milan

11 *Young Girl* (detail)
1943, bronze, height $52\frac{1}{2}$ in (133 cm)
Nelly Bär collection, Zürich

12 *Small Rider*
1944, bronze, $14\frac{1}{2} \times 16$ in (37×41 cm)
Louis D. Cohen collection, New York

13 *Juggler*
1944, bronze, height $34\frac{1}{4}$ in (92 cm)
Rollier collection, Milan

14 *Portrait of Georg Schmidt*
1945, polychrome plaster, height $14\frac{1}{4}$ in (36 cm)
Kunstmuseum, Basel

15 *Juggler*
1946, polychrome bronze, height 72 in (183 cm)
Werner and Nelly Bär collection, Zürich

16 *Small Rider*
1946, bronze, base $11 \times 8\frac{3}{4}$ in (28×22 cm) height $20\frac{1}{2}$ in (52 cm)
Museum of Modern Art, Kyoto

17 *Rider* (detail)
1947, bronze, height about $43\frac{1}{4}$ in (110 cm)
Pietro Campilli collection, Rome

18 *Rider*
1947, bronze, base $8\frac{1}{4} \times 11\frac{3}{4}$ in (21×30 cm) height $35\frac{1}{2}$ in (90 cm)
Grandjean collection, Zürich

19 *Rider*
1947, bronze, height $40\frac{1}{4}$ in (102 cm)
Stedelijk Museum, Amsterdam

20–21 *Rider* (detail)
1943, bronze, length $48\frac{1}{4}$ in (124 cm) height 45 in (114 cm)
Jesi collection, Milan

22 *Ersilia*
1930–49, polychrome wood, height 58 in (147 cm)
Kunsthaus, Zürich

23 *Ersilia* (detail)
1930–49

24 *Dancer*
1949, polychrome bronze, height $68\frac{1}{2}$ in (174 cm)
Wilhelm Lehmbruck Museum, Duisburg

25 *Small Rider*
1949, polychrome bronze, base $7 \times 9\frac{1}{2}$ in (18×24 cm)
height $17\frac{1}{4}$ in (44 cm)
Hirshhorn collection, Greenwich, U.S.A.

26 *Dancer*
1949, bronze, height 46 in (117 cm)
Werner and Nelly Bär collection, Zürich

27 *Portrait of Hermann Haller*
1949, polychrome plaster, height $13\frac{3}{4}$ in (35 cm)
Kunsthaus, Zürich

28 *Portrait of Igor Stravinsky*
1951, bronze, height $12\frac{1}{2}$ in (32 cm)
Kunstmuseum, Essen

29 *Rider*
1952–3, bronze, height 84 in (213 cm)
Nelly Bär collection, Zürich

30 *Dancer*
1953, polychrome plaster, height 66 in (168 cm)
Property of the artist, Milan

31 *Miracle* (detail)
1954, polychrome wood, base $28\frac{3}{4} \times 64\frac{1}{2}$ in (73×164 cm)
height $46\frac{1}{2}$ in (118 cm)
Kunstmuseum, Basel

32 *Miracle* (detail)
1954

33 *Warrior* (detail)
1959–60, polychrome plaster, base 67×45 in (170×114 cm)
height 53 in (135 cm)
Property of the artist, Milan

34 *The Set*
1960, oil on canvas, $74\frac{3}{4} \times 74\frac{3}{4}$ in (190×190 cm)
Property of the artist

35 *Juggler for a Stage Play*
1962, mixed techniques on canvas, $47\frac{1}{4} \times 59$ in (120×150 cm)
Marina Marini collection, Milan

36 *Portrait of Marc Chagall*
1962, bronze, height $11\frac{1}{2}$ in (29 cm)
Nelly Bär collection, Zürich

37 *The Encounter*
1951–66, oil on canvas,
$79\frac{1}{2} \times 47\frac{1}{2}$ in (202×121 cm)
Property of the artist, Milan

38 *The Dream*
1951–66, tempera on canvas, $47\frac{1}{4} \times 59$ in (120×150 cm)
Property of the artist, Milan

39 *A Form in an Idea*
1966, bronze, height $79\frac{1}{2}$ in (202 cm)
Property of the artist, Milan

40 *Warrior*
1967, stone, $173\frac{1}{4} \times 141\frac{3}{4}$ in (440×360 cm)
Property of the artist, Milan

Biographical notes

Marino Marini was born in a house in Piazza San Pietro, Pistoia, on 27th February 1901. He followed courses in painting and sculpture at the Florence Accademia di Belle Arti as a pupil of Domenica Trentacoste. After an initial period devoted to painting and drawing (though a few heads were modelled even at this early date in Marinian history), he began his proper role as sculptor in 1928 with *The Blind Man. The People*, probably the first work in which the features of his personal style are first fully established, dates from the following year. From 1929 to 1940 he held the chair in sculpture at the Sculoa d'Arte in Monza, succeeding Arturo Martini. These were the years of wide travel and decisive cultural experiences: frequently in Paris (where he met De Chirico, De Pisis, Campigli, Tanguy, Picasso, Braque, Gonzalez, Laurens, Magnelli), to Germany, Holland and England.

In 1938 he married Mercedes Pedrazzini, called by himself and his friends Marina as if to recognise in the name the harmony of feeling which has been and is one of the constant themes of the sculptor's life. In 1940 he left teaching in Monza for the chair of sculpture at the Accademia di Brera.

During the war he lived in Canton Ticino, in Switzerland where he met Giacometti, Wotruba, la Richier, Haller and Banninger. Returning to Italy in 1946, he settled finally in Milan, alternating between periods at his house in Piazza Mirabello and long summer holidays in the Germinia at Forte dei Marmi, with frequent visits to his house near Locarno. In 1950 he had his first exhibition in the United States, at the Curt Valentin Gallery in New York, and on this occasion met Arp, Calder, Lipchitz, Beckman and Feininger. On his return journey he stayed in England where he got to know Henry Moore whom he was later to see in Forte, where the English sculptor also spent his summers.

In 1952 he was given the Grand Prize for Sculpture at the Venice Biennale, in 1954 the Feltrinelli Prize from the Accademia dei Lincei, in 1957 he was elected to the Accademia di San Luca and in 1961 became a member of the Insigne Accademia Pintificia. Amongst his outstanding exhibitions we may count the two great collections at the Kunsthaus in Zürich in 1962, and the Palazzo Venezia, Rome in 1966.

29. Marino Marini with Henry Moore

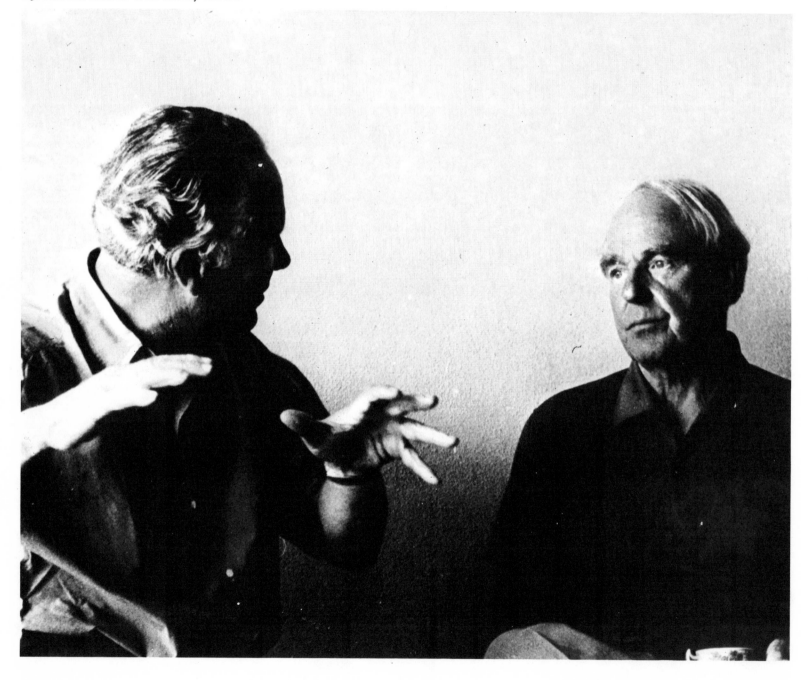

Chronological catalogue of works

1927. *Girl from Algiers* (oil on wood), property of the artist
1928. *The Sick Girl* (bronze), Peroni collection, Milan; *The Blind Man* (bronze), Galleria d'Arte Moderna, Florence; *Cristina* (bronze), Peroni collection, Milan; private collection, Florence
1929. *People* (terracotta), property of the artist; *Bather* (terracotta), Galleria Civica, Milan; *Portrait of Sensani* (bronze), private collection, Milan
1930. *The Townswoman* (terracotta), property of the artist; *Self-portrait* (plaster), Galleria Comunale d'Arte Moderna, Rome; *Portrait of Magnelli* (bronze), property of the artist; *The Musician* (marble), private collection, Rome; *The Sleeper* (terracotta), Galleria d'Arte Moderna, Rome; *Bust of a Woman* (terracotta), Gabriolo collection, Milan; *Seated Girl* (bronze, formerly also a plaster, now lost, and two terracottas dated 1933 and 1935), private collection, Turin
1930–49. *Ersilia* (wood), Kunsthaus, Zürich (the original plaster of 1930–1 and terracotta version were lost in the Second World War. The wooden work in Zürich was continued at various times until 1949)
1931. *Swimmer* (wood), private collection, Milan
1932. *Portrait of a Boy* (terracotta), property of the artist; *Portrait of a Girl* (terracotta), private collection, Milan; *Composition* (bronze), Jesi collection, Milan; M. Goldman collection, London
1933. *Juggler* (terracotta), Avetta collection, Alassio; *Portrait of Mrs Worms* (bronze), private collection, Paris; *Icarus* (wood), Battiato collection, Milan; *Portrait of a Woman* (plaster), private collection, Milan; *Portrait of P. Borra* (plaster), Borra collection, Milan; *New Queen*, five bas-reliefs (plaster), destroyed; *Young Girl* (terracotta), Barbaroux collection, Milan (variant in terracotta), property of the artist
1934. *Gaby* (stone), Cardazzo collection, Venice; *Portrait of Mrs Allen* (plaster), private collection, Milan; *Young Woman* (stone), Barbaroux collection, Milan; *Bacchus* (stone), Kunsthaus, Zürich; *Portrait of B. Baslini* (plaster), private collection, Milan; *Paola* (stone), Peroni collection, Milan; *Boxer* (bronze), Galleria d'Arte Moderna, Turin
1935. *Sketch for a Boxer* (bronze), J. Wade collection, New York; R.D.S. May collection, London; J. Butler collection, New York; *Boxer* (wood), Jeu de Paume, Paris; *Nude* (terracotta), property of the artist; *Portrait of A. Funi* (plaster), Funi collection, Milan; (variant in terracotta), private collection; *Bather* (stone), private collection, Rome; (variant in terracotta), Giani collection, Milan; *Rider* (bronze), Della Ragione collection, Genoa; *Reclining Pomona* (bronze), Jesi collection, Milan; and two versions in American collections
1936. *Boxer* (bronze), Institute of Fine Art, Detroit; *Young Woman* (terracotta), property of the artist; *Portrait of a Man* (terracotta), Galleria d'Arte Moderna, Rome; *Portrait of Signora Verga* (terracotta), de Lambert collection, Brussels; *Portrait of Fossati Bellani* (bronze), Fossati collection, Milan; *Portrait of Vecchi, the lawyer* (terracotta), Mucchi collection, Milan (variant in wood); *Rider* (bronze), Jesi collection, Milan; (variant in wood), Battiato collection, Verona; *Juggler* (plaster), private collection, Milan; Marelli collection, Milan
1937. *Man on Horseback* (bronze), Nationalmuseum, Stockholm; *Horse* (bronze), Della Ragione collection, Genoa; *Head of a Woman* (terracotta), Battiato collection, Verona; *Portrait of a Woman* (terracotta), Jesi collection, Milan; *Boxer* (bronze), private collection, Milan; *Portrait of the sculptor Melotti* (wax), Jesi collection, Milan; (variant in bronze), Mattioli collection, Milan; *Portrait of Lamberto Vitali* (stone), Mattioli collection, Milan; (variant in plaster), L. Lionni collection, Philadelphia
1938. *Young Girl* (bronze), property of the artist; (variant in terracotta), Jesi collection, Milan; *Portrait of Signora Vitali* (bronze), Vitali collection, Milan; (variant in stone), private collection, Genoa; *Juggler* (bronze), property of the artist (the relevant plaster, too); Landesgalerie, Hanover; Kunstmuseum, Basel; (variant in terracotta), Marelli collection, Milan; *Portrait of the lawyer Valdameri* (bronze), Valdameri collection, Milan
1939. *The Pilgrim* (bronze), Jesi collection, Milan; *Horse* (bronze), Pizzacaro collection, Milan; (variant in terracotta), Bagnoli collection, Milan; *Horse* (bronze), Mattioli collection, Milan; Bär collection, Zürich; De Sola collection, San Salvador; *Young Girl* (bronze), Jesi collection, Milan; *Portrait of Marina* (wax), property of the artist
1940. Four high-reliefs (plaster), Battiato collection, Verona; *Youth* (plaster), Zoia collection, Milan; *Composition* (plaster), property of the artist; *Pomona* (bronze), Jesi collection, Milan; *Juggler* (bronze), property of the artist; Musées Royaux, Brussels
1941. *Pomona* (bronze), Jesi collection, Milan; (variant, one headless, one lacking an arm, in bronze and plaster respectively), Musées Royaux, Brussels, and property of the artist; *Gianni* (plaster), private collection, Locarno; *Donatella* (plaster), property of the artist; *Portrait of De Pisis* (bronze), private collection, Stockholm; (plaster), property of the artist
1942. *Horse* (plaster), property of the artist; *Horse* (bronze), Curt Valentin Gallery, New York; *Nude* (plaster), Olsen collection, Oslo; *Man Hanged* (plaster), Baumann collection, Lugano; *Bather* (bronze), Curt Valentin Gallery, New York; *Venus* (bronze), Furer collection, Zürich; Tannahill collection, Detroit; *The Girl Friends* (terracotta), private collection, Rome; *The Dream of Venus* (plaster), property of the artist; *Reclining Nude* (plaster), property of the artist; *Pomona* (plaster), private collection, Milan; *Self portrait* (plaster), property of the artist; *Portrait of Campigli* (bronze), property of the artist; Throne-Holst collection, Stockholm; (plaster), Campigli collection, Paris; *Portrait of P. Pedrazzini* (bronze), private collection, Locarno; *Portrait of A. Tosi* (plaster), Jesi collection, Milan; (bronze), Vismara collection, Kunstmuseum, Basel
1943. *Young Girl* (bronze), W. & N. Bär collection, Zürich; *Three Small Pomonas* (bronze), private collection, Milan; Curt Valentin Gallery, New York; *Figure of a Woman* (plaster), property of the artist; *The Dream of Venus* (plaster), property of the artist; *Susanna* (bronze), Hirshhorn collection, Toronto; Phihl collection, Göteborg; *The Lady's Walk* (bronze), property of the artist; *Small Pomona* (bronze), property of the artist; Rockefeller collection, New York; Hillman collection, New York; Yale University, New Haven; *The Three Graces* (bronze), Rockefeller collection, New York; Curt Valentin Gallery, New York; *Small Rider* (plaster), property of the artist; *Nude* (bronze), Fontana collection, Milan; *Portrait of Mr Amsler* (plaster), Amsler collection, Schaffhausen; (bronze), Kunstverein, Winterthur; *Portrait of Signora Pedrazzini* (plaster), property of the artist; *Portrait of Signora Melms* (plaster), property of the artist; *Portrait of Marina* (bronze), property of the artist; Normann collection, New York; Ferber collection, Zürich; *Archangel* (plaster), property of the artist; (bronze), Konsthallen, Helsinfors; *The Miracle* (plaster), Jesi collection, Milan
1944. *Kneeling Nude* (plaster), property of the artist; *Small Rider* (bronze), L. D. Cohen collection, New York; *Dancer* (bronze), property of the artist; *Seated Juggler* (bronze), property of the artist; Penn collection, Philadelphia; Rollier collection, Milan; *Seated Figure* (bronze), Wadsworth Atheneum, Hartford; *Small Dancer* (bronze), property of the artist; private collection, London; *Portrait of N. Gasser* (plaster), property of the artist; (variant), Gasser collection, London; *Portrait of N. Bolla Martinez* (plaster), Bolla collection, Bellinzona; *Portrait of Mrs Hahnloser* (plaster), Hahnloser collection, Winterthur; *Portrait of Mme Baumann* (terracotta), property of the artist
1945. *Venus* (terracotta), Mattioli collection, Milan; *Judith* (bronze), Musée Royal des Beaux-Arts, Antwerp; *Pomona* (cement), property of the artist; *Pomona* (bronze), private collection, Rome; City Museum, Bochum; *Pomona* (stone), W. & N. Bär collection, Zürich; *Nude* (bronze), D. Westman collection, Stockholm; Cincinnati Art Museum, Cincinnati; *Nude* (bronze), Landesgalerie, Hanover; Morlotti collection, Milan; *Dancer* (bronze), Tanzi collection, Milan; (variant), Bertoletti collection, Rome; *Quadriga* (bronze), Curt Valentin Gallery, New York; *Horse* (painted plaster), von Schumacher collection, Lucerne; *Rider* (bronze, bas-relief), Zeltuer collection, Zürich; *Rider* (bronze), Nationalmuseum, Göteborg; E. Hilton collection, London; *Portrait of a Man* (cement), Buhrer Sulzer collection, Schaffhausen; *Portrait of Lamberto Vitali* (bronze), Vitali collection, Milan; Museum of Modern Art, New York; S. A. Lewison collection, New York; (variant in plaster), Jesi collection, Milan; *Portrait of Baron von Schumacher* (coloured plaster), von Schumacher collection, Lucerne; *Portrait of a Woman* (coloured plaster), property of the artist; *Fiorenza* (plaster), property of the artist; *Portrait of Germaine Richier* (coloured plaster), property of the artist; *Portrait of Emanuel Gasser* (coloured terracotta), property of the artist; (bronze), P. T. Nielsen collection, Copenhagen; *Portrait of Mme Grandjean* (coloured plaster), Grandjean collection, Zürich
1946. *Rider* (coloured plaster), property of the artist; (bronzes), J. Heller collection, Bethesda, U.S.A.; Hanover Gallery, London; Frua De Angeli collection, Milan; *Horse* (coloured plaster), property of the artist; *Horse* (bronze), Campanini collection, Milan; R. Colin collection, New York; Haas collection, San Francisco; *Seated Pomona* (bronze), property of the artist; *Juggler* (bronze), Bär collection, Zürich; Galleria d'Arte Moderna, Rome; Art Institute, Chicago; (one version in coloured plaster and another in bronze), property of the artist; *Portrait of Carlo Carrà* (lead), Jesi collection, Milan; (bronze), Museo Civico, Trieste; Osborn college, Salisbury; (plaster), property of the artist
1947. *Sketch for a Rider* (bronze), Schnelling collection, London; *Rider* (bronze), Campilli collection, Rome; *Horse and Rider* (bronze), Grandjean collection, Zürich; Art Museum, Portland; J. T. Soby collection, Farmington; Lee Ault collection, New Canaan; Butler collection, New York; *Rider* (bronze), Boymans-van-Beuningen Museum, Rotterdam; Tate Gallery, London; J. D. Rockefeller collection, New York; *Rider* (bronze), R. Jucker collection, Milan; Blanden Art Gallery, Fort Dodge, U.S.A.; Museum of Fine Art, Houston; *Rider* (coloured wood), private collection, Turin; *Rider* (wood), Curt Valentin Gallery, New York; *Rider* (polished plaster), property of the artist; (bronzes), Museum of Modern Art, New York; S. Marx collection, Chicago; Stedelijk Museum, Amsterdam; Stadtmuseum, Cologne; *Pomona* (bronze), Jesi collection, Milan; *Pomona* (bronze), property of the artist; L. N. Cohen collection, Chicago; C. Faerber collection, Göteborg; A. Ryan, Bridge of Allan, Scotland; *Nude* (bronze), Jucker collection, Milan; *Nude* (bronze), Curt Valentin Gallery, New York; Malcolm Brush collection, London; *Portrait of Richard Jucker* (coloured plaster), Jucker collection, Milan; *Portrait of Dada Pizzocaro* (coloured plaster), Pizzocaro collection, Milan; *Portrait of Mrs Jeker* (lead), Jeker collection, Milan; *Portrait of Judith Campigli* (coloured plaster), property of the artist; *Portrait of Emilio Jesi* (bronze), Jesi collection, Milan; *Portrait of James Dunn* (plaster), property of the artist; *Portrait* (lead), Sven Ericson collection, Stockholm
1948. *Rider* (bronze), Jesi collection, Milan; *Rider* (bronze), Curt Valentin Gallery, New York; R. Davis collection, Wayzata, U.S.A.; V. S. Schram collection, Burlington, U.S.A.; *Portrait of Mrs Soby* (bronze), J. T. Soby collection, Farmington; *Portrait of Paolo Lampugnani* (bronze), Lampugnani collection, Milan; *Portrait of Sognora Scalini* (terracotta), Scalini collection, Milan
1949. *Rider* (bronze), Marina Marini collection, Milan; Curt Valentin Gallery, New York; A. Ryan collection, Bridge of Allan, Scotland; J. Hirshhorn collection, New York; Hutchinson collection, East Bergholt, England; *Rider* (bronze), Jesi collection, Milan; *Rider* (bronze), A. Korner collection, London; P. Watson collection, London; A. Jeffress collection, London; *Small Rider* (bronze), L. Stern collection, New York; *Small Rider* (bronze), B. Watson collection, New York; R. Colin collection, New York; Saidenberg collection, New York; L. Block collection, Chicago; J. S. Newberry collection, Detroit; *Rider* (bronze), City Art Museum, St. Louis; Walter Arts Centre, Minneapolis; S. Ingersoll collection,

Philadelphia; *Rider* (wood), Kunstverein, Dusseldorf; *Pomona* (bronze), Gemeentmuseum, The Hague; Statensmuseum, Copenhagen; Walker collection, London; *Studies for Pomona* (bronzes), property of the artist; *Nude* (bronze), Jucker collection, Milan; von Celsing collection, Stockholm; S. A. Lewisohn collection, New York; *Dancer* (bronze), Wilhelm Lehmbruck Museum, Duisberg; (variants), Curt Valentin Gallery, New York; J. T. Soby collection, New Canaan; *Dancer* (bronze), Galleria d'Arte Moderna, Milan; W. & N. Bär collection, Zürich; Hanover Gallery, London; *Portrait of Mrs Fischer* (bronze), Fischer collection, New York; *Portrait of H. Haller* (coloured plaster), Kunsthaus, Zürich

1949–50. *Rider* (bronze), P. Guggenheim collection, Venice; E. Kaufmann collection, Pittsburg; *Rider* (wood), H. Krayenbuhl collection, Zürich

1950. *Four Studies for a Rider* (bronzes), property of the artist; *Sketch for a Rider* (bronze), A. Scueltzer collection; L. Feininger collection, New York; W. Lundington collection, Santa Barbara, California; J. Cowles collection, Minneapolis; *Small Horse* (bronze), Hanover Gallery, London; Estorick collection, London; Frank Perls Gallery, Beverley Hills; H. Pihl collection, Göteborg; *Horse* (bronze), Pierre Matisse Gallery, New York; F. Stenton collection, New York; McFadden Harrison collection, New York; J. Temple collection, Chicago; Bechtler collection, Zürich; *Horse* (bronze), Kunsthalle, Hamburg; Bechtler collection, Zürich; E. Kauffmann collection, Bear Run, U.S.A.; Toledo Museum of Art, Toledo, U.S.A.; *Portrait of Igor Stravinsky* (bronze), Museum of Art, San Francisco; *Portrait of the Architect Harrison* (bronze), Rockefeller collection, New York; *Portrait of Nelson Rockefeller* (bronze), Rockefeller collection, New York; *Portrait of H. Gates Lloyd*, Lloyd collection, Haverford; *Portrait of Monique* (bronze), B. Watson collection, New York; *Three Pomonas* (oil on canvas), private collection, Rome; *Parade I* (oil on paper), Toninelli collection, Milan; *Rider and Acrobat* (mixed techniques on paper), Galerie d'Art Moderne, Basel

1951. *Small Horse* (bronze), Frua collection, Milan; J. L. Plaza collection, Caracas; *Small Rider* (bronze), Frank Perls gallery, Beverley Hills; B. McLean collection, Dallas; J. Z. Steinberg collection, Chicago; S. Maslon collection, Wayzala, U.S.A.; *Small Horse* (bronze), Curt Valentin Gallery, New York; C. Lennart collection, New York; *Rider* (bronze), Hanover Gallery, London; Raynar Miltzan Skeppsredare, Oslo; Manufacturers Trust Company, New York; L. Florsheim collection, Chicago; *Rider* (coloured plaster), D. Thompson collection, Pittsburgh; (bronze), Estorick collection, London; A. Biberg collection, Göteborg; de Lambert collection, Brussels; *Rider* (bronze), Galleria La Medusa, Rome; Hirshhorn collection, Greenwich, U.S.A.; Faeber collection, Göteborg; Galeria Berggruen, Paris; Macchiati collection, Milan; *Horse* (bronze), property of the artist; R. Jucker collection, Milan; Bernouilli collection, Basel; Rusche collection, Cologne; M. d'Arquian collection, Brussels; R. Lamberson collection, New York; *Horse* (bronze), Marabon collection, Stockholm; N. A. Rockefeller collection, New York; F. Matarazzo Sobrinho collection, Sao Paulo, Brazil; *Small Bull* (bronze), Hanover Gallery, London; Cramer Gallery, Geneva; Saidenberg Gallery, New York; (coloured plaster), property of the artist; *Rider and Juggler* (oil on canvas), Kunsthalle, Bern

1951–2. *The Miracle* (bronze), property of the artist; Middelheim Museum, Antwerp; Hanover Gallery, London; Olson Foundation, Guilford Island, U.S.A.

1952. *Small Rider* (bronze), I. Coca collection, New York; Frank Perls gallery, Beverley Hills; H. Cutting collection, Chicago; C. Faeber collection, Göteborg; Galerie der Spiegel, Cologne; private collection, Düsseldorf; *Horse* (bronze), property of the artist; H. Oldquist collection, Stockholm; T. Ahrenberg collection, Stockholm; S. W. Marsch collection, New York; *Horse* (bronze), Hanover Gallery, London; Windfohr collection, Fort Worth, U.S.A.; R. Hodgson collection, New Canaan; Stein collection, Cologne; *Dancer* (bronze), Koninkljik Museum, Antwerp; de Lambert collection, Brussels; A. Long collection, New York; *Parade III* (oil on canvas), private collection, Rome; *Red Horse* (oil on canvas), A. M. Mess collection, Noorwjikerout; *Horse* (oil on canvas), Kröller-Müller Museum, Otterlo; *Falling Game* (oil on canvas), private collection, Locarno; *Azure Rider* (oil on canvas), W. Herdeg collection, Zürich

1952–3. *Rider* (bronze), W. & N. Bär collection, Zürich; J. Hirshhorn collection, New York; *Rider* (coloured wood), Kröller-Müller Museum, Otterlo

1953. *Sketch for a Rider* (bronze), Rosengart Galerie, Lucerne; Galerie Berggruen, Paris; Sanders collection, Rotterdam; Pierre Matisse Gallery, New York; Curt Valentin Gallery, New York; J. Hirshhorn collection, New York; R. T. Schoelkopt collection, New York; *Rider* (bronze), Curt Valentin Gallery, New York; Galerie d'Art Modern, Basel; *Bull* (bronze), Museo de Arte Moderna, Rio de Janeiro; Pierre Matisse Gallery, New York; Curt Valentin Gallery, New York; *Juggler* (bronze), Pierre Matisse Gallery, New York; H. Cutting collection, Chicago; G. Cramer Gallery, Geneva; *Juggler* (bronze), Hanover Gallery, London; G. Cramer Gallery, Geneva; Pierre Matisse Gallery, New York; G. Lenart collection, New York; *Juggler* (bronze), H. Moller collection, New York; *Jugglers* (bronze), Pierre Matisse Gallery, New York; Saidenberg Gallery, New York; G. Cramer Gallery, Geneva; *Acrobats* (bronze), Bechtler collection, Zürich; Pierre Matisse Gallery, New York; Curt Valentin Gallery, New York; C. Goodyear collection, New York; A. Morgenthan collection, New York; Rosengart Gallery, Lucerne; Galerie Vormel, Düsseldorf; *Dancer* (bronze), Bechtler collection, Zürich; Albright Art Gallery, Buffalo, U.S.A.; (lead), Jesi collection, Milan; (coloured plaster), property of the artist; *Small Dancer* (bronze), Hanover Gallery, London; G. Cramer Gallery, Geneva; Rosengart Gallery, Lucerne; M. Erlanger collection, New York; *Study for the Miracle* (bronze), Pierre Matisse Gallery, New York; *Portrait of Manfred von Mautner Markhof* (bronze), von Mautner Markhof collection, Vienna; (coloured plaster), property of the artist; *The Contemplatives* (oil on canvas), Jesi collection, Milan; *The Warriors and the Dance* (oil on canvas), Wemberg collection, Zürich; *Acrobats* (oil on masonite), Devoto-Falk collection, Milan

1953–4. *Large Miracle* (polished plaster), property of the artist; (bronze), Stadtische Kunstheim, Mannheim; Rotterdam (monument to the martyrs of the war), Museum of Modern Art, New York; *Study for the Miracle* (bronze), Jesi collection, Milan; Kunstmuseum, Winterthur; Max Wanerman collection, New York; *The Miracle* (bronze), Kunsthistorisches Museum, Vienna; Palais des Beaux-Arts, Charleroi; Institute of Arts, Baltimore; *Acrobats and Jugglers* (coloured bronzes), property of the artist

1954. *Small Rider* (bronze), Vormel Galerie, Düsseldorf; *Small Juggler* (bronze), property of the artist; Hanover Gallery, London; Galerie Berggmen, Paris; Pierre Matisse Gallery, New York; J. Hirshholm collection, New York; *Portrait of Curt Valentin* (bronze), property of the artist; Museum of Modern Art, New York; Kunsthalle, Hamburg; *Portrait of Lucy de Lambert* (coloured bronze), property of the artist; de Lambert collection, Brussels; *The Miracle* (coloured wood), Kunstmuseum, Basel; *Equestrian composition* (oil on canvas), private collection, Lugarno; *Riders Game* (oil on masonite), private collection, Rome; *Fall of the Rider* (oil on masonite), Guarini collection, Milan

1955. *The Idea of the Rider* (bronze), property of the artist; *Rider* (bronze), Hanover Gallery, London; Galerie Berggmen, Paris; Pierre Matisse Gallery, New York; *Small Miracle* (bronze), Galerie Rosengart, Lucerne; G. Cramer Gallerie, Geneva; Galerie Vormel, Düsseldorf; *Portrait of Countess Seefried* (lead), L. Schnitzler collection, Frankfurt; *Limit of Imagination* (oil on canvas), I. Troubetzkoi collection, Paris; *The Promise* (oil on canvas), Toninelli collection, Milan; *Study for the Miracle* (mixed styles on paper), private collection, Milan; *Study for the Miracle* (tempera on *reframed* paper), property of the artist; *Invocation* (oil on canvas), Boymans-von-Beuningen Museum, Rotterdam; *Horse in Harmony* (oil on paper), A. Mondadori collection, Camaiore

1955–6. *Rider* (bronze), property of the artist; Galerie d'Art Moderne, Basel; Galerie Rosengart, Lucerne; Galerie Berggruen, Paris; Pierre Matisse Gallery, New York; *Study for a Small Miracle* (bronze), property of the artist; Galerie Rosengart, Lucerne; Pierre Matisse Gallery, New York; *The Warrior* (coloured wood), property of the artist

1956. *The Idea of the Rider* (coloured wood), property of the artist; *Warrior* (bronze), property of the artist; *Composition* (bronze), Hanover Gallery, London; Pierre Matisse Gallery, New York; *Composition* (bronze), Hanover Gallery, London; *Composition* (bronze), Galerie d'Art Moderne, Basel; Hanover Gallery, London; *Composition* (bronze), Galerie G. Cramer, Geneva; *The Juggler* (oil on canvas), W. H. Rudhart collection, Essen Bredeney; *Orpheus* (oil on canvas), property of the artist; *Theatrical Farce* (oil on canvas), private collection, Milan

1956–7. *Rider* (bronze), Bechtler collection, Zürich; Shell building, London; P. Marinotti collection, Milan; *Rider* (bronze), Bauwlust, The Hague; *The Miracle* (bronze), property of the artist; *Heroic Imagination* (oil on canvas), Toninelli collection, Milan

1957. *Sketch for the Miracle* (bronze), property of the artist; *Representation in Blue* (oil on canvas), private collection, Rome; *Study of Forms* (oil on paper), private collection, Locarno

1958. *The Miracle* (mixed techniques on paper), Toninelli collection, Milan; *The Idea of the Rider I* (oil on paper), private collection, Locarno; *Representation in Green* (oil on canvas), Jesi collection, Milan; *A Vision of Figures* (oil on paper), Jesi collection, Milan; *Theatrical Rapture* (oil on paper), Jesi collection, Milan

1958–9. *The Miracle* (coloured wood), Civica Galleria d'Arte Moderna, Turin; (bronze), Kunsthaus, Zürich; Bayerische Staatliche Gemäldesammlungen, Munich; Jesi collection, Milan

1959. *The Warrior* (bronze), R. Jucker collection, Milan; Germanisches Nationalmuseum, Nuremberg; *Pomona* (mixed technique on paper), Toninelli collection, Milan

1958–60. *Large Theatre* (oil on canvas), private collection, Rome

1959–60. *The Warrior* (bronze), property of the artist; T. Weiner collection, Fort Worth, U.S.A.; *The Orchestra* (oil on canvas), S. Cinicola collection, Milan; *Pomona* (mixed techniques on paper), M. Dell'Acqua collection, Milan

1960. *Composition for the Miracle* (bronze), property of the artist; *Composition of Elements* (bronze), property of the artist; *Portrait of Siegfried Rosengart* (bronze), Galerie Rosengart, Lucerne; property of the artist; *Study for the Rider* (mixed techniques on paper), private collection, Milan; *The Idea II* (varnish on paper), private collection, Milan; *Iberia* (mixed techniques on backed paper), A. Blum collection, Locarno; *The Warrior II* (oil on paper), private collection, Milan; *The Scenario* (oil on canvas), property of the artist

1961. *Portrait of Henry Miller* (coloured plaster), property of the artist; six bronze castings in various American collections; *Detail of the Warrior* (oil on paper), Toninelli collection, Milan; *Liveliness in Play* (oil on paper), private collection, Darmstadt

1961–3. *The Cry* (oil on paper), Toninelli collection, Milan

1962. *Sketch for the Cry* (bronze), property of the artist; private collections in Canada and Sweden; *The Cry* (bronze), property of the artist; *Portrait of Professor Carl Georg Heise* (bronze), property of the artist; *Portrait of Jean Arp* (plaster), property of the artist; *Portrait of Henry Moore* (coloured plaster), property of the artist; *Portrait of Marc Chagall* (bronze), Nelly Bär collection, Zürich; *Juggler for a Play* (mixed techniques on canvas), Marina Marini collection, Milan

1963. *The Cry* (bronze), property of the artist; *Composition of Elements* (bronze), Bo Boustedt Collection, Kungalv, Sweden; *Composition of Elements II* (mixed techniques on backed paper), Toninelli collection, Milan; *Composition of Elements III* (oil on backed paper), Toninelli collection, Milan; *Composition of Elements IV* (mixed techniques on backed paper), Toninelli collection, Milan; *Live Music* (oil on canvas), Toninelli collection, Milan; *Spell of the Dancers* (oil on canvas), Toninelli collection, Milan

1963–4. *Composition of Elements* (bronze), property of the artist

1964–5. *Composition of Elements* (bronze), property of the artist

1965. *Composition of Elements* (tempera on paper), property of the artist

1951–66. *The Encounter* (oil on canvas), property of the artist; *The Dream* (tempera on canvas), property of the artist
1966. *A Form in an Idea* (bronze), property of the artist
1967. *Warrior* (stone), property of the artist; *Portrait of Mies Van der Rohe* (bronze), National Galerie, Berlin; property of the artist; *Portrait of Gottfried B. Fischer* (bronze), Fischer collection, Camaiore

Exhibitions and catalogues

Here follows a chronological list of the shows and exhibitions in which Marini has participated. For easier reference we have chosen to omit articles written in catalogues from the general bibliography and to insert them in italics here, beside the shows to which the catalogues refer. Thus the reader will easily be able to follow the story of the critical reception of these shows, as the development of Marini's work itself. By turning, then, to the bibliography for the articles that appeared in periodicals, he will gain as complete a picture as possible of the critical reaction to Marini year by year.

1923. Rome. II Biennale Romana.
1927. Monza. III Mostra Internazionale delle Arti Decorative (May–October).
1928. Milan. Gruppo del Novecento Toscano. Galleria Milano (December). *Cat. by Raffaele Franchi.*
1929. Nice. Exposition du Novecento Italiano à la Société des Beaux Arts (March–April). *Cat. by Antonio Maraini.* Paris. Exposition d'Art Italien Moderne aux Editions Bonaparte (30th November). *Cat. by Mario Tozzi.* Milan. Il Mostra del Novecento Italiano (2nd March–30th April).
1930. Berne. Die Entwicklung der Modernen Kunst in Italien. Kunstmuseum (March–May). Basel. Ausstellung Moderne Italiener in der Kunsthalle (5th–12th February).
1931. Stockholm. Mostra del Novecento Italiano (9th September–4th October). *Cat. by Margherita Sarfatti.*
1932. Milan. Galleria Milano (February). Rome. Galleria Sabatello (6th–13th November). Venice. XVIII Esposizione Internazionale d'Arte.
1933. Milan. Mostra di Campigli e Marini. Galleria Milano.
1934. Geneva. Exposition d'Art Italien à Génève. (22nd September–18th November). *Cat. by G. de Reynolds.* Venice. XIX Esposizione Internazionale d'Arte.
1935. Vienna. Italienischer Plastik der Gegenwart (November). *Cat. by Leo Planiscig.* Rome. II Quadriennale d'Arte Nazionale.
1937. Milan. Galleria Barbaroux (December).
1940. Zürich. Ausstellung Zeitgenössicher Italienischer Maler und Bildhauer. Kunsthaus (November–December). *Cat. by Antonio Maraini.*
1941. Genoa. Galleria Genova (March).
1942. Rome. Galleria dello Zodiaco (30th November). *Cat. by Filippo de Pisis.*
1943. Venice. Galleria del Cavallino.
1944. Basel. Vier auslanische Bildhauer in der Schweiz. Kunstmuseum (14th October–26th November).
1945. Berne. Marino Marini, Germaine Richer, Fritz Wotruba. Kunsthalle (9th June–8th July). Basel. Galerie d'Art Moderne (9th September–5th October). Zürich. Galerie Aktuaryus (26th September–17th October). *Cat. by Lamberto Vitali.*
1947. Lucerne. 40 Jahre Italienischer Kunst. Kunstmuseum (29th March–1st June). Lausanne. Quarante ans d'Art Italien. Musée Cantonal des Beaux Arts (15th February–15th March). *Cat. by Giovanni Ponti.*
1948. New York. Sculpture. Buchholz Gallery (28th September–16th October). Venice. Biennale (sala personale). Stockholm. Italiensk Nutidskonst Färg och Form (September). *Cat. by Giuseppe Galassi.* Göteborg. Italiensk Nutidskonst. Konstmuseet (October). *Cat. by Giuseppe Galassi.* Madrid. Exposicion de Arte Italiano Contemporaneo (May).
1949. Palm Beach. Rodin to Brancusi. Society of the Four Arts (4th–27th March). New York. Exhibition of 20th Century Italian Art. Museum of Art. *Cat. by Soby-Barr.* Milan. Collezione Peggy Guggenheim. Palazzo Reale (June–July). *Cat. by Francesco Flora.* Rome. Galleria dell'Obelisco (18th March). *Cat. by Palma Bucarelli.* Philadelphia. 3rd Sculpture International Fairmount Park Art Association. *Cat. by Ellen Phillips S. Memorial.* Catania and Palermo. Mostra d'Arte Contemporanea. Circolo Artistico.
1950. Brussels. Art Italien Contemporain. Palais des Beaux Arts (28th January–28th February). *Cat. by Giuseppe Raimondi.* New York. Buchholz Gallery (Curt Valentin) (14th February–11th March). *Cat. by James Thrall Soby.* Washington. 35 drawings Marino Marini. Watkins Gallery (2nd–24th March). Munich. Werke Europäischer Plastik. Haus der Kunst (1st November–24th December).
1951. London. Marino Marini. Sculpture and Drawings. Hanover Gallery (8th May–16th June). *Cat. by James Thrall Soby.* London. Sculpture. Battersea Park 1951 (May–September). *Cat. by Ruth Dalton.* Antwerp. Exposition Inaugural du Musée Communal de sculpture en plein air. Middleheim (8th September–31st October). Winterthur. Die Plastiksammlung Werner Bär. Kunstmuseum (16th September–11th November). *Cat. by Hermann Hubacher.*
1951–2. Hanover. Kestner Gesellschaft. *Cat. by Alfred Hentzen.*
1952. Munich. Bayerische Staatsgemäldesammlungen, Haus der Kunst (21st March–4th May). *Cat. by Berhard Degenhart.* Venice. Biennale (sala personale) (June–September). Cincinnati. Second International Biennal of Contemporary Color Lithographs. The Cincinnati Art Museum. *Cat. by Gustave von Groschwitz.* Hamburg. Kunstverein. *Cat. by Alfred Hentzen.* Salzburg. Marini, Moore, Wotruba. Galerie Welz. *Cat. by Ernst Köller.* Arnhem. Sonsbeck '52. Internationale Tentoonstelling. Beeldhouwkunst (30th May–15th September). *Cat. by J. A. de Goeijen.* Recklinghausen. Ausstellung Mensch und Form unserer Zeit. Stadtische Kunsthalle (13th June–3rd August). *Cat. by Franz Grosse Perdekamp.* Chicago. Contemporary Drawings 1945–1952. The Art Institute of Chicago. *Cat. by Carl O. Schwniewind.* Philadelphia. Sculpture of the twentieth century. Philadelphia Museum of Art. Fairmount Park Art Association (11th October–7th December).
1953. Göteborg. Kunstmuseum (January–February). *Cat. by Christian Faerber.*

Chicago. Sculpture of the twentieth century. The Art Institute of Chicago (22nd January–8th March). Stockholm. Swenks Franska Konstgalleriet (February–March). *Cat. by Christian Faerber.* Copenhagen. Statens Museum for Kunst (14th March–7th April). *Cat. by Christian Faerber.* Cincinnati. Cincinnati Art Museum (April–May). Oslo. Nasjonalgalleriet (April–May). *Cat. by Christian Faerber.* Toukokun. Italiensk mälarkonst skulptur grafik. Tadehalli. Konsthallen (May). *Cat. by Umbro Apollonio.* Hamburg. Plastik im freien (30th April–31st October). *Cat. by Werner Haftmann.* New York. Sculpture of the twentieth century. The Museum of Modern Art (29th April–7th September). *Cat. by Andrew C. Ritchie.* Ostend. Art Fantastique. Kursaal (5th July–31st August). *Cat. by Emile Langui.* New York. Curt Valentin Gallery (27th October–21st November). *Cat. by Sinagra.* Houston. Seventy-five years of Sculpture. Museum of Fine Art (November).

1953–4. Zürich. Junge Italienische Kunst. Kunsthaus (21st November–10th January). *Cat. by R. Wehrli.* São Paulo, Brazil. II Biennale.

1954. Ohio. Contemporary Sculptor's drawings. The School of Fine and Applied Arts. The Ohio State University. *Cat. by Joseph Schwarz.* Helsinki. Galerie Artek (26th January–16th February). *Cat. by Umbro Apollonio.* Geneva. Galerie Gérald Cramer (1st March–1st April). Berne. Gutekunst und Klipstein (13th–28th April). Cologne. Galerie der Spiegel (May–June). *Cat. by Eduard Trier.* Basel. Galerie d'Art Moderne (29th May–15th July). London. Sculpture in the open air. Holland Park (May–September). Zürich. Galerie 16 (29th November–24th December). São Paulo, Brazil. La segunda Bienal de São Paulo. Futuristas e artistas italianos de hoye. *Cat. by Rodolfo Pallucchini.*

1955. Rotterdam. Museum Boymans (26th February–28th April). *Cat. by A. M. Hammacher.* Düsseldorf. Kunstverein (8th May–12th June). Mannheim. Kunsthalle (25th June–31st July). *Cat. by Walter Passage.* Stad Antwerpen. III Biennale. Middelheim park. *Cat. by L. Craeybeck.* Paris. Galerie Berggruen (30th September–29th October). *Cat. by Douglas Cooper.* New York. Martha Jackson Gallery (October). *Cat. by Dority Norman.* Hamburg. Farbige Lithographien. Galerie Hoffmann (November). New York. Spring Exhibition. P. Matisse Gallery (2nd–28th May). Recklinghausen. Das Bild des Menschen. Städt Kunsthalle (12th June–26th July). Pittsburgh. The 1955 Pittsburgh International Exhibition of Contemporary Painting. Carnegie Institute (October–December). *Cat. by Gordon B. Washburn.* Kassel. Documenta. Internationale Ausstellung. Museum Friderianum (15th July–18th September). *Cat. by Werner Haftmann.* St. Louis. Contemporary Italian Art. City Art Museum of St. Louis (13th October–14th November). *Cat. by W. N. Eisendrath jr.* New York. First showing of recent works. Pierre Matisse Gallery (December).

1956. London. Modern Italian Art from the Estorick Collection. The Arts Council of Great Britain. *Cat. by Philip James.* Paris. Exposition Internationale de sculpture contemporaine. Musée Rodin. *Cat. by Paul Leon.* London. The Hanover Gallery (8th May–16th June). *Cat. by James Thrall Soby.* New York. Rodin to Lipchitz. Fine Arts Associates (9th October–3rd November). *Cat. by John Coolidge.* Recklinghausen. International Ausstellung (January).

1957. Buffalo (New York). Contemporary Art. Albright Art Gallery. Buffalo Gallery. *Cat. by Gordon M. Smith.* Munich. Arte Italiana dal 1910 ad oggi. Haus der Kunst (6th June–15th September). *Cat. by Fortunato Bellonzi.* Erlangen Orangerie. Graphik des 20 Jahrhunderts aus Erlangen. Privatbesitz (20th February–31st March). *Cat. by Bernhard Meyer Rutz.* Düsseldorf. Bronzen und Bilder von Marino Marini. Galerie Vömel (10th March–30th April). *Cat. by Christoph Bernouilli.* New York. The Contemporaries (1st–20th April). Baden-Baden. Ausstellung. 'Il Miracolo'. Kunsthalle (August–September). *Cat. by Mahlow.* Messina. Scultura Italiana del XX secolo (1st August–15th September). *Cat. by Giovanni Carandente.* Rome. Scultura Italiana del XX secolo (November–December). *Cat. by Giovanni Carandente.*

1957–8. Bologna. Scultura Italiana XX secolo (22nd December–3rd January). *Cat. by Giovanni Carandente.* Chicago. Italian Sculptors. The Arts Club of Chicago (10th December–23rd January). New York. Sculpture 1880–1957. Fine Arts Associates (10th December–11th January).

1958. New York. Marini, sculpture, paintings. P. Matisse Gallery (11th–29th March). Brussels. Exposition Universelle et Internationale de Bruxelles. '50 ans d'Art Moderne' (17th April–12th July). *Cat. by Em. Langui.* Antwerp. La sculture dans la ville (June–August). London. Giacometti, Marini, Matisse, Moore. The Hanover Gallery (24th June–13th September). Lausanne. Galerie Valotton (June–July). Caracas. Morandi, Tosi, Marino Marini, Campigli, Sironi. Galeria de Arte Contemporaneo (12th September). *Cat. by Edgardo Giorgi Alberti.* Zürich. Le Corbusier, Marino Marini. Galerie Palette (18th July). Cleveland. Some contemporary works of art. The Cleveland Museum of Art. *Cat. by Shermann and Lee.* Duisburg. Bildhauer. Zeichnungen des 20-Jahrhunderts. Stadtisches Kunstmuseum (1st–30th March). *Cat. by G. Händler.*

1958–9. Pittsburgh. Exhibition of Contemporary Painting and Sculpture. Carnegie Institute Pittsburgh (5th December–8th February). *Cat. by Gordon B. Washburn.*

1959. Antwerp. V Biennale Middelheim. *Cat. by L. Craeybeckx.* Eskilstuna Stad. Skulptur i Miljo (18th May–28th June). *Cat. by Svante Lundkvist.* Kassel. II Documenta. Internationale Ausstellung (11th July–11th October). *Cat. by Werner Haftmann. Cat. by E. Trier.* Venice. Vitalità nell'arte. Esposizione Internazionale. Palazzo Grassi (August–September). *Cat. by Henry Michaux.* Zürich. Werner Baer plastik. Kunsthaus (August–September). *Cat. by Werner and Nelly Bär.* Berne. Plastiksammlungen Werner Baer. Kunstmuseum (26th September–15th November). *Cat. by Hugo Wagner.* Otterlo. Tekeningen van Beeldhouwers 19e en 20e eeuw. Rijksmuseum Kröller-Müller (13th June–2nd August). *Cat. by A. M. Hammacher.* Recklinghausen. Vitalità nell'arte. Kunsthalle (October–December). The sculpture collection of Mr and Mrs Ted Weiner. Fort Worth Art Center (5th–25th October). *Cat. by Henry B. Caldwell.* Michigan. The 1959 Purchase Exhibition. Kresge Art Center. Michigan State University (November). *Cat. by Allen Leepa and Howard Church.* Raleigh. Masterpieces of Art. North Carolina Museum of Art (6th April–17th May). *Cat. by James B. Byrnes.*

1959–60. Düsseldorf. Italienische Aquarelle und Zeichnungen der Gegenwart. Kunsthalle (18th December–17th January). *Cat. by Bernhard Degenhart.* Amsterdam. Vitalità nell'arte. Stedelijk Museum (December–January).

1960. Tokyo. Lithographs by Marino Marini. The National Museum of Modern Art. (29th January–21st February). *Cat. by Atsuo Imaizumi.* Rotterdam. Beeldententoostelling Floriade. Museum Boymans van Beuningen (25th March–25th September). Erlangen Orangerie. Marino Marini, Zeichnungen, Gouachen, Litographien (17th–20th April). Milan. Arte Italiana del XX secolo da Collezioni Americane. Palazzo Reale (30th April–26th June). *Cat. by James Thrall Soby.* Basel. La femme. Galerie Beyler (May–June). Rome. Arte Italiana del XX secolo da Collezioni Americane. Museo d'Arte Moderna (July–August).

1961. New York. The James Thrall Soby Collection. The Museum of Modern Art (1st–25th February). *Cat. by Alfred H. Barr jr.* Scultura Italiana. Museo d'Arte Moderna (February). Tokyo. The VI Tokyo Biennale. *Cat. by Tsynelaka Beda.* Stad Antwerpen. 6 Biennale voor Beeldhouwkunst. Middleheim (15th July–15th October). *Cat. by L. Craeybeckx.*

1961–2. Pittsburgh. The Pittsburgh International Exhibition. Carnegie Institute (27th October–7th January). *Cat. by Gordon B. Washburn.*

1962. Basel. Sommer Ausstellung. Gallerie d'Art Moderne. London. International Exhibition of Contemporary Art. The O'Hana Gallery (15th–24th November). *Cat. by Herbert Read.* Frankfurt. Marino Marini, gouachen und lithographien. Galerie Vonderbank (January). Zürich. Kunsthaus (23rd January–25th February). *Cat. by Eduard Hüttinger.* Art since 1950. Seattle World's Fair 1962 (2nd April–21st October). *Cat. by Sam Hunter.* Spoleto. Esposizione Internazionale di scultura nella città di Spoleto (June–September). Venice. Biennale. Vienna. Kunst von 1900 bis Heute. Museum des XX Jahrhunderts (21st September–4th November). *Cat. by Werner Hofmann.*

1962–3. Zürich. Eroffnungausstellung. Gimpel und Hanover Galerie (November–5th January).

1963. Milan. Proposta per una raccolta d'Arte Moderna. Galleria Toninelli (23rd January). *Cat. by Guido Ballo.* Ivrea. Disegni Italiani Moderni. Centro Culturale Olivetti (February). *Cat. by Giovanni Carandente.* Tokyo. Symposium International de la Sculpture Moderne au Japon. Museum of Modern Art. *Cat. by Soichi Tominaga.* Basel. Arp, Calder, Marini. Galerie d'Art Moderne (11th May–30th September). Darmstadt. Zeugnisse in der Angst in der Modernen Kunst. Mathildenhohe (29th June–1st September). *Cat. by Hans Gerhart Evers.* Göteborg. Skulptur. Bo Boustedts Samling. Göteborgs Konstmuseum (29th August–6th October). *Cat. by Alfred Westholm.*

1963–4. Milan. Marino Marini, dipinti. Galleria Toninelli (November–February). *Cat. by Frano Russoli.* Milan. Scrittori della Scuola di Milano. Centro Culturale Pirelli (14th December–12th January). *Cat. by Marco Onorato.*

1964. Milan. Idea e spazio, acqueforti di Marino Marini, Galleria Ciranna (28th February–26th March). Basel. Synthèse. Galerie d'Art Moderne (16th June–30th September). London. Painting and Sculpture of a Decade organised by the Calouste Gulbenkian Foundation at the Tate Gallery (22nd April–28th June). Lugano. Bianco e Nero. VIII Esposizione Internazionale. *Cat. by Giuseppe Martinola.* Lausanne. Chefs d'Oeuvres des Collections Suisses. Palais de Beaulieu (1st May–25th October). Munich. Bilhauerzeichnungen. Galerie Günther Franke (8th June–15th July). Lübeck. Moderne Skulptur. Bo Boustedts Sammlung. Dommuseum (4th July–2nd August). *Cat. by Alfred Westholm.* Rotterdam. Marino Marini als Schilder. Museum Boymans van Beuningen (6th November–6th December). *Cat. by Raffaele Carrieri.* New York. The Artist's Reality. An International Sculpture Exhibition. New School Art Center (14th October–14th November). *Cat. by Paul Mocsanyi.* Darmstadt. Internationale der Zeichnung. Mathildenhöhe (12th September–15th November). *Cat. by H. W. Sabais.* Philadelphia. Curatorial Retrospective. Philadelphia Museum of Art (21st September–1st November). *Cat. by Carl Zigrosser.* Munich. Marino Marini als Maler. Günther Franke Galerie (25th April–30th May). *Cat. by Werner Haftmann.* Venice. XXXII Biennale Internazionale d'Arte. Turin. Mostra di scultura in metallo. Galleria Civica d'Arte Moderna. (19th September–18th October). *Cat. by C. C. Anselmetti.* Kassel. Documenta III (27th June–5th October). *Cat. by Werner Haftmann.*

1964–5. Pittsburgh. Pittsburgh International Museum of Art. Carnegie Institute (30th October–10th January). *Cat. by Gustave von Groschwitz.*

1965. Stad Antwerpen. Marino Marini als schilder. Koninklijk Museum voor Schöne Kunsten (27th February–19th April). *Cat. by Lode Craeybeckx.* Hamburg. Religiose Kunst unserer Zeit. St. Jacob Kirche. Hamburger Kunsthalle (3rd February–7th March). *Cat. by Certrude Schiller.* Milan. Afro, Burri, Marino. Toninelli Arte Moderna (4th March–5th April). Amsterdam. Grandes sculptures d'aujourd'hui. Vondelpark (1st April–1st October). *Cat. by Sandberg.* Jerusalem. The Billy Rose Art Garden. The Israel Museum (2nd May–2nd November). Milan. Scultura Europea. Galleria d'Arte Annunciata (14th April–5th May). *Cat. by Mario de Micheli.* Zürich. Aquarelle und Zeichnungen von Marino Marini. Galerie Obere Zäune (29th April–29th May). Milan. Litografie rare di Marino Marini. Galleria Ciranna (30th September–29th October). Hanover. Sammlung Sprengel. Kunstverein (10th October–28th November). *Cat. by Alfred Hentzen.* Athens. Panathenées de la Sculpture Mondiale (8th September–8th November). Milan. V Fiera del Disegno. Galleria d'Arte Annunciata. Odense. Skulpture i Eventyrhaven International Skulptur. Stattuetter i Radhushallen (19th June–31st August). *Cat. by Jan Zibrandtsen.*

1965–6. Wellington. Contemporary Italian Sculpture. A Queen Elizabeth II Arts Council exhibition. Auckland (September–January). *Cat. by Fortunato Bellonzi.* London. L'Atelier Mourlot. Redfern Gallery (7th December–31st January).

Cat. by Jean Adhémar. Philadelphia. Marino Marini. Graphics and Related Works. Philadelphia Museum of Art (3rd December–16th January). *Cat. by Giovanni Carandente*.

1966. Rome. Palazzo Venezia (10th March–10th June). *Cat. by Giovanni Carandente*. Milan. La Figura. Toninelli Arte Moderna (30th March–30th April). Darmstadt. Marino Marini als Maler und Graphiker. Kunsthalle (21st May–3rd July). *Cat. by Werner Haftmann*. Turin. La Figura. Galleria Narciso (14th May–16th June). Florence. Forma e Verità I. Palazzo Capponi (7th–30th May). *Cat. by Lorenzo Papi*. Arnhem. 5e Internationale Beeldentoonstelling. Sonsbeek '66 (27th May–25th September). *Cat. by. H. L. C. Jaffé*. Mexico. Arte Italiano Contemporaneo Museo de Arte Moderno. *Cat. by Fortunato Bellonzi*. Nuremberg. Marino Marini als Maler und Graphiker. Fränkische Galerie am Marientor (4th September–9th October). *Cat. by Werner Haftmann*. Erlangen Orangerie. Plastik in unserer Zeit (13th November–4th December). *Cat. by Helmut Lederer*. Kaiserslautern. Marino Marini als Maler und Graphiker. Pfalzgalerie (15th October–15th November). *Cat. by Werner Haftmann*.

1966–7. Milan. Alcuni aspetti della Pittura Contemporanea. Toninelli Arte Moderna (December–January).

1967. Milan. La Figura. Toninelli Arte Moderna (24th February–20th March). Florence. Arte Moderna in Italia 1915–1935. Palazzo Strozzi (26th February–28th June). *Cat. by C. L. Ragghianti*. Paris. Orangerie. Chefs d'Œuvres des Collections Suisses (May). *Cat. by Jean Chatelan, F. Damte, Hélène Adremar*. Montreal. International Exhibition of Contemporary Sculpture. Expo 67. *Cat. by Guy Robert*. Milan. Marino Marini, Mostra di dipinti inediti. Toninelli Arte Moderna (October–November). Milan. Da Picasso a Guttuso. Galleria Annunciata (21st October–10th November). Vancouver. Exposition Internationale de Gravure a Vancouver. The Vancouver Art Gallery (5th–29th October). *Cat. by William S. Lieberman*. Turin. Capolavori. Galleria La Bussola (December).

1967–8. New York. Sculpture from Twenty Nations. Guggenhei.n International Exhibition. Guggenheim Museum (20th October–4th February). *Cat. by Edward F. Fry*. Pittsburgh. The 1967 Pittsburgh International Exhibition of Contemporary Painting and Sculpture. Carnegie Institute (27th October–7th January). *Cat. by Gustave von Groschwitz*. New York. First showings of paintings, sculpture, drawings. Pierre Matisse Gallery (19th December–25th January).

1968. Stockholm. Marino Marini. Färglitografier. Italienska Kulturinstitutet (23rd April–4th May). Pistoia. Mostra fotografica. Sculture di Marino Marini. Da Valiani (8th June–8th August). *Cat. by Corrado Gelli and Arrigo Valiani*.

Bibliography

MONOGRAPHS

P. FIERENS, *Marino Marini*, Art Italien Moderne, Croniques du Jour, Paris-Hoepli, Milan, 1936; H. FUCHS, *Il Miracolo di Marino Marini*, Philipp Reclam jr., Stuttgart, 1963; L. VITALI, *Marino Marini*, Arte Moderna Italiana, n. 29, Hoepli, Milan, 1937; G. CESETTI, *Marino Marini*, Quaderni del Disegno, Ed. del Cavallino, Venice, 1939; F. DE PISIS, *Marino Marini presentato da F. d. P.*, Ed. della Conchiglia, Milan, 1941; L. ANCESCHI, *Marino Marini*, Quaderni del disegno contemporaneo, 'Galleria della Spiga e Corrente', Milan, 1942; G. CONTINI, *20 sculture di Marino Marini*, Ed. della Collana, Lugano, 1944; L. VITALI, *Marini*, Quaderni d'Arte a cura di G. Raimondi e di C. L. Ragghianti, Ed. U, Florence, 1946; R. CARRIERI, *Marino Marini*, Ed. del Milione, Milan, 1948; E. CARLI, *Marino Marini*, Arte Moderna Italiana, n. 29, Hoepli, Milan, 1950; M. RAMOUS, *Marino Marini*, Cappelli, Bologna, 1951; ID., *Marino Marini, du litografie e sei disegni*, Cappelli, Bologna, 1951; U. APOLLONIO, *Marino Marini*, Ed. del Milione, Milan, 1953, 2nd ed. revised *ibidem.*, 1958; E. TRIER, *Marino Marini*, Galerie der Spiegel, Cologne, 1954; SINAGRA (pseudonym of Egle Marini), *Marino, sei tavole a colori*, Ed. del Milione, Milan, 1954; E. LANGUI, *Marini*, Allert de Lange, Amsterdam, 1954; D. COOPER, *Marino Marini*, Silvana editoriale d'arte, Milan, 1959; E. MARINI, *Marino Marini*, der Arche, Zürich, 1959; P. M. BARDI, *Marini, Graphic Work and Paintings*, Harry N. Abrams, New York, 1960; W. HOFMANN, *Marini, Malerei und Graphik*, Gerd Hatje, Stuttgart, 1960; ID., *L'Opera Grafica di Marino Marini*, Il Saggiatore, Milan, 1960; E. MARINI, *Marino Marini, Ein Lebensbild. Ein Gespräch mit seiner Schwerter Egle*. Fischer Bücherei, Frankfurt, 1961; E. TRIER, *Marino Marini*, Gerd Hatje, Stuttgart, 1961; ID., *Marino Marini*, Garzanti, Milan, 1961; ID., *Marino Marini*, Editions du Griffon, Neuchatel, 1961; ID., *Marino Marini*, Praeger, New York, 1961; ID., *Marino Marini*, Thames & Hudson, London, 1961; F. RUSSOLI, *Il Guerriero di Marino Marini*, Aldo Martello, Milan, 1963; ID., *Marino Marini, dipinte e disegni*, Toninelli, Milan, 1963; ID., *Marino Marini, paintings and drawings*, Harry N. Abrams, New York, 1965; G. CARANDENTE, *Le Litografie di Marino Marini*, Toninelli, Milan, 1966.

ARTICLES FROM BOOKS AND PERIODICALS

R. FRANCHI, *Mostra toscana novecentesca*, 'L'Illustrazione Toscana', November 1926; R. FONDI, *Marino Marini, incisore e scultore*, 'Rassegna Grafica', November–December 1927; R. FRANCHI, *La Mostra del sindacato artistico*, 'L'Illustrazione Toscana', May 1927; R. PACINI, *La prima mostra d'arte provinciale a Pistoia*, 'Il Raduno', January 1928; R. CALZINI, *La XVI Biennale di Venezia*, 'Emporium', September 1928; R. FRANCHI, *I pistoiesi in Mostra*, 'L'Illustrazione Toscana', February 1928; M. TINTI, *La scultura alla II Mostra dei sindacati toscani*, 'L'Italia Letteraria', May 1929; P. TORRIANO, *Aspetti dell'Arte Moderna Italiana–Lombardi e Toscani*, 'L'Illustrazione Italiana', February 1929; S. VOLTA, *Il Novecento*, 'Il Selvaggio', Florence, March 1929; V. COSTANTINI, *Alla XVII Biennale di Venezia*, 'L'Italia Letteraria', June 1930; F. FOSCA, *Une exposition d'Art Italien Moderne*, 'L'amour de l'Art', Paris, February 1930; F. SAPORI, *Alla XVII Biennale veneziana*, 'Rasegna dell'Istruzione artistica', Urbino, August 1930; *Pittori e scultori toscani a Venezia*, 'L'Arca', Milan, August 1930; A. SARTORIS, *Die Entwicklung der modernen Kunst in Italien*, 'Kunstler des Neuen Italien', Berne, March 1930; N. BERTOCCHI, *Alla I Quadriennale*, 'L'Italia Letteraria', April 1931; D. BROGI, *Visita a Marino Marini*, 'L'Illustrazione Toscana', April 1931; G. SCHEIWILLER, *Gang durch die erste Quadriennale d'Arte nazionale in Rom* (manuscript), 1931; C. CARRA, *Alla XVIII Biennale di Venezia–La scultura*, 'L'Ambrosiano', Milan, 22nd June 1932; A. FRANCINI, *Scultura italiana d'ieri e d'oggi*, 'L'Italia Letteraria', 22nd June 1932; U. OJETTI, *La XVIII Biennale a Venezia–Gli scultori italiani*, 'Corriere della Sera', Milan, 12th May 1932; E. C. OPPO, *Sculture e pitture di Marino Marini*, 'La Tribuna', Rome, 16th November 1932; A. PODESTA, *Come si presenta la scultura italiana alla Biennale*, 'Il Secolo XIX', Genoa, 29th April 1932; E. N. ROGERS, *Mostre milanesi–Marino Marini*, 'L'Italia Letteria', 17th April 1932; M. RUDEL, *Artisti italiani: Marino Marini*, 'Augusto', Rome, 15th November 1932; L. VITALI, *L'Arte italiana alla Biennale di Venezia*, 'Domus', Milan, June 1932; E. ALKMAN, *Italiensk mutidskonst*, 'Göteborgs Posten', Göteborg, 10th July 1932; V. BUCCI, *Una Mostra di Marino Marini*, 'Il Corriere della Sera', Milan, 9th February 1932; M. BIANCALE, *Mostre romane d'Arte–Marino Marini*, 'Il Popolo di Roma', 10th November 1932; R. CARRIERI, *L' Accademia del Risotto*, 'Cronaca Prealpina', Varese, 10th February 1933; G. PENSABENE, *La scultura alla Quadriennale*, 'Il Quadrivio', Rome, 24th February 1933; N. BERTOCCHI, *Alla XIX Biennale*, 'L'Italia Letteraria', Rome, 14th July 1934; L. BOLGIANI, *Mostre milanesi–Marino Marini*, 'Quadrivio', Rome, 4th February 1934; D. BONARDI, *Artisti che espongono: Marini*, 'La Sera', Milan, 16th January 1934; V. BUCCI, *Artisti che espongono: Marini*, 'Il Corriere della Sera', Milan, 10th January 1934; R. CALZINI, *Ventennio 1914–1934*, 'L'Italia', Milan, 1934; C. CARRA, *Mostre d'Arte*, 'L'Ambrosiano', Milan, 10th January 1934; ID., *Gli scultori italiani alla Biennale*, 'L'Ambrosiano', Milan, 6th September 1934; R. CARRIERI, *Studi di pittori*, 'L'Eco del Mondo', Rome, 3rd November 1934; A. DEL MASSA, *La XIX Biennale veneziana–Della coerenza stilistica e della scultura*, 'La Nazione', Florence, 19th May 1934; B. BECCA, *Marino Marini*, 'Corriere Padano', Ferrara, 4th May 1935; N. BERTOCCHI, *La seconda Quadriennale Romana–Parole agli idolatri*, 'Il Frontespizio', Florence, July 1935; E. CECCHI, *La seconda Quadriennale*, 'Circoli', Rome, May 1935; V. COSTANTINI, *I grandi Premi–Marino Marini*, 'La Sera', 11th June 1935; L. DE LIBERO, *Stato dell'arte italiana contemporanea alla II Quadriennale*, 'Broletto', Como, March 1935; G. GORGERINO, *I premi di 100,000 lire alla Quadriennale–Severini e Marini*, 'L'Ambrosiano', 2nd May 1935; A. LANCELOTTI, *Alla Quadriennale–Marini e Ruggeri*, 'Roma', Naples, 20th February 1935; L. LANZA, *Lo scultore Marino Marini*, 'Circoli', March–April 1935; A. MARIANI, *Ricordi della Mostra di Parigi–La nuova sala italiana al Jeu de Paume*, 'L'Illustrazione Italiana', Milan, 29th December 1935; G. MARCHIORI, *La seconda Quadriennale–La scultura italiana*, 'Corriere Padano', 26th February 1935; ID., *Marino Marini vince un premio alla Quadriennale*, 'Il Commercio Pistoiese', Pistoia, 8th June 1935; R. MELLI, *Visita ad artisti–Marino Marini*, 'Il Quadrivio', Rome, 7th April 1935; E. MASELLI, *La scultura alla II Quadriennale d'Arte*, 'L'Italia Letteraria', Rome, 20th April 1935; G. PENSABENE, *La scultura alla Quadriennale*, 'Il Quadrivio', Rome, 24th February 1935; R. G. M., *La Quadriennale romana*, 'Eve', Milan, 16th February 1935; P. RIZZO, *La scultura alla II Quadriennale d'Arte–Marino Marini*, 'L'Ora', Palermo, 18th February 1935; P. TORRIANO, *La II Quadriennale d'Arte Nazionale–Scultura*, 'L'Illustrazione Italiana', Milan, 31st March 1935; L. VITALI, *Ancora la II Quadriennale romana*, 'Domus', Milan, May 1935; E. ZANZI, *Il pittore Severini e lo scultore Marino Marini vincitori dei premi di 100,000 lire alla II Quadriennale*, 'La Gazzetta del Popolo', Turin, 12th April 1935; G. WALDEMAR, *L'Art Italien au XIX et au XX Siècle de l'Exposition de Paris*, 'La Renaissance', Paris, 1935; ID., *La Quadriennale de Rome*, 'L'Art et les Artistes', Paris, March 1935; N. BERTOCCHI, *La XX Biennale–La scultura italiana*, 'L'Italia Letteraria', Rome, 12th July 1936; L. BORGESE, *Venti firme dell'Arte Italiana vivente*, 'Il Convegno', Milan, 25th February 1936; C. CARRA, *Scultori italiani e stranieri alla XX Biennale di Venezia*, 'L'Ambrosiano', 2nd August 1936; A. DEL MASSA, *La Mostra d'Arte del sindacato toscano*, 'L'Illustrazione Toscana', June 1936; R. FRANCHI, *Disegni all'Accademia artistica fiorentina*, 'L'Italia Letteraria', 21st June 1936; U. OJETTI, *La XX Biennale veneziana–Scultori nostri*, 'Corriere della Sera', 5th July 1936; E. C. OPPO, *Alla XX Biennale di Venezia–Due scultori diversissimi fra loro*, 'La Tribuna', 29th July 1936; D. TERRA, *Lineamenti della XX Biennale–L'Arte Italiana*, 'Il Quadrivio', Rome, 7th June 1936; N. BERTOCCHI, *Uno scultore moderno e il suo critico*, 'Il Popolo d'Italia', Milan, 13th July 1937; C. CARRA, *Mostre d'Arte: la collettiva del Milione*, 'L'Ambrosiano', Milan, 5th February 1937; C. G. MARCHESINI, *Libri d'Arte–Marino Marini*, 'Corriere Padano', 9th December 1937; L. VITALI, *Marino Marini*, 'Arte Moderna Italiana', Milan, 1937; F. DE PISIS, *Marino Marini*, 'Il Meridiano di Roma', 7th November 1937; ID., *Marino Marini*, 'Prose e Articoli', Milan, 1937; P. FIERENS, *Le drame de la Biennale*, 'XX Siècle', Paris, July–August–September 1938; M. MARINI, *Cavallo e cavaliere*, 'Broletto', Como, May 1938; D. MOROSINI, *Sculture di Marino Marini*, 'Corrente di vita giovanile', Milan, 15th December 1938; G. MARCHIORI, *Caratteri e forme della scultura italiana alla XXI Biennal di Venezia–Marino Marini*, 'Corriere Padano', 15th July 1938; ID., *Libri d'Arte–Marino Marini*, 'Corriere Padano', 6th February 1938; M. MARINI, *Spiegazioni*, 'L'Ambrosiano', Milan, 26th May 1938; ID., *Grande Arte Moderna*, 'Provincia di Como', 29th June 1938; P. FIERENS, *Sculpture–Marino Marini*, 'XX Siècle', Paris, March 1939; *Le Arti in Italia*, 'Domus', Milan, 1939; G. CESETTI, *Disegni di Marino Marini*, 'Il Meridiano di Roma', 19th November 1939; M. MARINI, *Le mie sculture*, 'Il Tempo', Rome, 14th December 1939; D. MOROSINI, *Disegni di Marino*, 'Corrente di vita giovanile', Milan, 30th November 1939; E. DELLA PURA, *Ritratti di Marini*, 'Le Arti', Rome, February–March 1939; G. MARCHIORI, *La Quadriennale di Roma*, 'Corriere Padano', 5th February 1939; G. PIOVENE, *Artisti che espongono, Marino Marini*, 'Corriere della Sera', 12th December 1939; M. BONTEMPELLI, *Arte Italiana contemporanea*, Milan, 1940; ER., *Moderne Italienische Kunst*, 'Die Tat', Zürich, 24th November 1940; *Marino Marini–Ritratto*, 'Domus', Milan, January 1940; *Moderne Italienische*, 'Die Nation', Berne, 28th November 1940; W. WARTMANN, *Marino Marini–Bacchus*, 'Zürcher Kunstgesellschaft', Annual, 1940; L. REPACI, *Mito moderno di Marino*, 'Stile', January 1941; RIVA, *Marino Marini*, 'Giornale di Genova', 23rd March 1941; G. VISENTINI, *Le Arti*, 'Il Popolo di Roma', 2nd April 1941; ID., *Le Sculture di Palazzo dell'Arte a Milano*, 'Il Popolo di Roma', 29th May 1941; V. COSTANTINI, *Dibattiti d'arte contemporanea*, 'Il Popolo d'Italia', 28th March 1941; G. PIOVENE, *La Mostra sindacale di Milano*, 'Primato', Rome, 15th June 1941; A. PODESTA, *La III Mostra Nazionale*, 'Il Secolo XIX', Genoa, 26th May 1941; P. I. A., *Novecento*, 'L'Eco di Bergamo', 19th April 1941; R. CALZINI, *Scultura e arti minori*, 'Il Popolo d'Italia', 6th June 1941; A. PODESTA, *Mafai e Marini a Genova*, 'Primato', Rome, 15th April 1941; M. RIZZOLI, *Mafai e Marino*, 'Corriere Mercantile', Genoa, 17th March 1941; P. V., *Marino Marini*, 'Meridiano di Roma', 25th May 1941; A. PODESTA, *Mafai e Marini*, 'Il SecoloXIX', Genoa, 26th March 1941; *Aus dem Zürcher Kunsthaus*, 'Neue Zürcher Zeitung', Zürich, 10th January 1941; G. CESETTI, *La collezione Cardazzo alla Galleria di Roma*, 'Corriere Padano', 16th April 1941; U. OJETTI, *Raccolte d'Arte*, 'Corriere della Sera', Milan, 17th January 1941; A. PEYROT, *Via degli Artisti*, 'Il Piccolo', 5th April 1941; ID., *Mostra Nazionale di Belle Arti*, 'Il Piccolo', 26th May 1941; G. PIOVENE, *Marino Marini*, 'Civiltà', 21st October 1942; E. DELLA GIOVANNA, *Marino Marini: scultore, pittore e vagabondo*, 'Stile', Milan, May 1942; *Maillot-Kolbe-Haller-Marini*, 'Schweizer Journal', Zürich, October 1942; G. C. ARGAN, *Marino Marini*, 'Almanacco', 'Beltempo', Rome, 1942; PODESTA, *Scultori italiani d'oggi–Evoluzioni di Marino*, 'L'Illustrazione Toscana', May 1942; E. MASTROLONARDO, *Mostre d'Arte a Roma*, 'Meridiano di Roma', 27th December 1942; R. GIOLLI, *Fermezza di Marino*, 'Domus', Milan, February 1943; E. ZANZI, *Cronache d'Arte–Profilo: Marino Marini*, 'L'Italiano', Turin, 27th March 1943; M. MASCIOTTA, *Marino Marini*, 'Letteratura', May–August 1943; *Umanità di tre opere di Marino alla Quadriennale*, 'Stile', Milano, May 1943; H. KELLER, *Vier ausländische Bildhauer in der Schweiz*, 'Werk', Winterthur, December 1944; KN., *Vier ausländische Bildhauer im Kunstmuseum*, 'National Zeitung', 16th October 1944; A. MOHLER, *Marino Marini*, 'Schweizer Monatshefte', Basel, December 1944; H. MILLER, *L'oscenità e la legge di riflessione*, page 22, Milan, 1944; L. VITALI, *Marino Marini*, 'Werk', Winterthur, November 1944; L. SARTORIS, *Marino Marini*, 'Svizzera Italiana', page 223, Lugano, June 1944; L. VISCONTI, *Marino Marini*, 'Corriere del Ticino', Lugano, 20th May 1944; R., *Sculture di Marino*, 'Libera Stampa', Lugano, 26th October 1944; G. SCHMIDT, *Vier ausländischer Bildhauer in der Schweiz*, 'Die Weltwoche', Zürich, 20th October 1944; EG., *Kunst in Basel*, 'Neue Zürcher Zeitung', Zürich, 31st October 1944; ME., *Vier ausländische Bildhauer in Kunstmuseum Basel*, 'Die Tat', 5th November 1944; G. V., *Marino Marini*, 'Giornale del Popolo', Lugano, 15th November 1944; A. B., *Ausländische Bildhauer in der Schweiz*, 'Luzerner Neueste Nachrichten', 3rd November 1944; C. S., *Vier ausländer Bildhauer im Kunstmuseum Basel*, 'St. Galler Tagblatt', St. Gallen, 25th November 1944; M. GASSER, *Zu einem verlorenen Blatt*, 'Die Weltwoche', Zürich, 10th November 1944; GG., *Ausstellung von vier ausländischen Bildhauern*, 'Basler Nachrichten', Basel, 16th October 1944; G. VIGORELLI, *Marino Marini*, 'Giornale del Popolo', Lugano, 15th November 1944; L. VITALI, *Marino Marini*, 'Corriere del Ticino', Lugano, 20th May 1944; W. A., *Plastik Ausstellung*, 'Bund', Berne, 16th June 1945; W. O., *Ausstellung Marino Marini*, 'Basler Volksblatt', Basel, 18th September 1945; E. BR., *Kunst in Zürich*, 'Bund Morgen Blatt', Berne, 8th October 1945; K., *Vingt sculptures de Marino Marini*, 'Werk', Winterthur, 9th September 1945; A. JANNER, *Marino Marini ritrattista*, 'Svizzera Italiana', Lugano, 30th January 1945; D. VALERI, *Marino Marini*, 'Servir', Lausanne, 5th January 1945; E. BR., *Moderne ausländische Bildhauer*, 'Neue Berner Zeitung', 2nd July 1945; H. W., *Marino Marini*, 'Die Weltwoche', Zürich, 21st September 1945; P. SCHAFFNER, *Wiedereröffnung des Basler Kunstmuseums*, 'Der Landbote', Winterthur, 21st September 1945; W. R., *Marino Marini*, 'Werk', Winterthur, November 1945; ME., *Drei in der Schweizlebende Italiener*, 'Die Tat', Zürich, 6th October 1945; U. FREY, *Figure e disegni di Marino Marini*, 'Libera Stampa', Lugano, 12th October 1945; R. CARRIERI, *Disegno Contemporaneo*, Milan, 1945; C. CARRA, *Marino Marini*, 'Lettere ed Arti', November 1945; H. W., *Ausstellung Marino Marini*, 'Basler Nachrichten', Basel, 13th September 1945; ME., *Moderne Plastik in Bern*, 'DieTat', 19th June 1945; NT., *Ausländische Plastik in Bern*, 'National Zeitung', Basel, 9th July 1945; NT., *Vernissage der Ausstellung Marino Marini*, 'National Zeitung', 10th September 1945; SINCERO, *Sculture di Marino*, 'Veneto Liberale', Venice, 19th November 1945; D. VALERI, *Marino Marini*, 'La Giostra', Milan, 25th October 1945; W. SULSER, *Marino Marini*, 'Kunst und Volk', Zürich, 1946; P. SALATI, *Marino Marini*, 'Libera Stampa', Lugano, 4th January 1946; P. BIANCONI, *Note su Marino*, 'Belle Lettere', Lugano, February 1946; A. M., *Bildhauerzeichnungen*, 'Die Weltwoche', Zürich, 11th October 1946; NT., *Eine Ausstellung von Bildhauerzeichnungen*, 'National Zeitung', 1st October 1946; NT., *Graphik zeitgenossischer Meister*, 'National Zeitung', 18th May 1946; F. CARASSO, *Inleiding bij Het Werk van Marino Marini*, 'Apollo', Kerstmis-Amsterdam, 1947; E. VITTORINI, *Nomi e statue a proposito dell'Arcangelo di Marino Marini*, 'Domus', April 1947; Milan, April 1947; R. CARRIERI, *Un fanciullo toccato dalla grazia di Venere*, 'Milano Sera', 27th December 1947; CAIROLA, *Marino Marini*, 'Omnibus', Milan, 11th February 1947; V. COSTANTINI, *Il sarcastico Marino*, 'Il Sabato Lombardo', Milan, 17th May 1947; E. VITTORINI, *Marino–Nomi e statue*, 'Politecnico', December 1947; R. CARRIERI, *Marini o del mito di Venere*, 'Tempo', Milan, 2nd August 1947; P. RICCI, *Pomona di Marino Marini*, 'La Voce', Naples, 26th June 1948; P. SALATI, *Luci e ombre alla Biennale di Venezia*, 'Libera Stampa', 25th June 1948; T. SCIALOIA, *Arti figurative*, 'Mercurio', Rome, June 1948; B. ZANI, *Commentiamo i premi*, 'Il Momento', Rome, 12th June 1948; R. GUTTUSO, *Alcuni artisti italiani e stranieri*, 'Rinascita', July 1948; G. MARUSSI, *La nuova scultura italiana, vera rivelazione della Biennale*, 'Gazzetta di Mantova', 22nd June 1948; M. RAMOUS, *Marini e Moore*, 'Il Progresso d'Italia', 2nd July 1948; G. MARUSSI, *Su tutte le opere straniere quelle italiane dominano*, 'Fronte Democratico', Cremona, 18th June 1948; P. BIANCONI, *Marino Marini*, 'Corriere del Ticino', Lugano, 25th June 1948; PAROS, *'Ni' sospeso a mezz'aria sulla statua di Marini*, 'Il Gazzettino', Venice, 26th June 1948; G. MARCHIORI, *Due scultori–Marini e Manzù*, 'Il Mattino del Popolo', 13th June 1948; R. CARRIERI, *Vernice*, 'Il Tempo', 19th June 1948; ID., *La Scultura alla Quadriennale*, 'Il Tempo', Milan, 24th April 1948; L. VITALI, *La scultura di Marino Marini*, 'La Provincia', Como, 10th April 1948; M. LEPORE, *A Venezia ha vinto il compromesso*, 'Milano Sera', 16th June 1948; M. RAMOUS, *Ha rischiato il suo cielo il toscano Marino Marini*, 'Il Progresso d'Italia', Bologna, 6th March 1948; A. S., *Ben venga la statua del Marini, ma senza diritti di riproduzioni*, 'Il Gazzettino', Venice, 26th February 1948; N. BERTOCCHI, *I capi mozzi di Marino Marini*, 'La Fiera Letteraria', Rome, 27th February 1948; R. CARLI-BALLOLA, *Marino Marini*, 'Avanti', Milan, 18th February 1948; F. FILIPPINI, *Meditazione sulla XXIV Biennale*, 'Svizzera Italiana', Locarno, August–October 1948; L. VITALI, *Marino Marini*, 'Horizon', London, September 1948; L. MILLER, *Venice Biennale*, 'Vogue', London, August 1948; R. CARRIERI, *Ossessione equina di Marino Marini*, 'Tempo', Milan, 8th–15th May 1948; G. MARCHIORI, *Marino Marini*, 'Vernice', Trieste, 21st March 1948; U. APOLLONIO, *Notizie delle Arti*, 'La Rassegna d'Italia', Milan, May 1948; G. MARCHIORI, *Due scultori: Marini e Manzù*, 'Il Mattino del Popolo', 13th June 1948; ID., *Marini e Manzù*, 'Ulisse', Rome, July 1948; M. VALSECCHI, *Per una statua Vicenza si accapiglia*, 'Oggi', Milan, 5th September 1948; M. EICHENBERGER, *Im Spiegel der Biennale Venedig 1948*, 'Du', Zürich, November 1948; J. T. SOBY, *The Venice Biennale*, 'The Saturday Review', New York, 7th August 1948; S. HUNTER, *European Sculpture*, 'The New York Times', 3rd October 1948; R. CARRIERI, *Tre 'Ma' dominano il campo*, Milan, 28th August 1948; F. CARASSO, *Italiaanse Plastik*, 'Kronick van Kunst en Kultur', February 1948; L. MANISCO, *Alla Biennale*, 'L'Italia Socialista', Rome, 17th June 1948; R. REBORA, *Armonia di contrasti*, 'L'Umanità', Milan, 12th June 1948; C. SEYMOUR JR., *Tradition and Experiment in Modern Sculpture*, Washington, 1949; L. VENTURI, *The new Italy arrives in America*, 'Art News', New York, 1949; G. A. DELL'ACQUA, *Posizione di Marino*, 'L'Ulivo', July–October 1949; *Marino Marini–Italiens Grosser lebender Bildhauer*, 'Heute', Munich, October 1949; J. T. SOBY, *Marino Marini who lives in Milan*, 'Saturday Review of Literature', 3rd December; R. R., *Intervista con Marino Marini*, 'La Voce d'Italia', Paris, 25th January 1949; M. VALSECCHI, *Lo scultore Marino Marini ha riaperto uno studio a Milano*, 'Oggi', Milan, 28th April 1949; P. BIANCONI,

Marino Marini, 'Corriere del Ticino', Lugano, 6th May 1949; F. B. ANNONI, *Tage bei Marino*, 'Die Weltwoche', Zürich, 30th September 1949; G. BALLO, *Sculture di Marino Marini*, 'Tempo', 2nd July 1949; C. BARONI, *Solitudine di Marino Marini*, 'Il Popolo', Milan, 19th August 1949; R. CARRIERI, *Pittura-Scultura d'avanguardia in Italia*, Milan, 1950; C. BRANDI, *Marino Marini*, 'L'Immagine', Rome, 1950; *Marino Marini–Sculptor from Italy becomes U.S. Best Seller*, 'Life', New York, May 1950; *Marini–The new Italy's top sculptor has his first U.S. show*, 'Look', New York, February 1950; B. KRASNE, *Maestro Marini*, 'The Art Digest', March 1950; *Talented Tuscan*, 'Newsweek', February 1950; *Marini*, 'Time', February 1950; G. EICHOFF, *Marino Marini*, 'Gronningen', Charlottenborg, January 1950; D. SECKLER, *This March of the Sculptors*, 'Art News', March 1950; L. VENTURI, *A propos de l'exposition de peinture et sculpture italiennes contemporaines*, 'Les Beaux Arts', Brussels, 1950; R. CARRIERI, *Marino e la 57a Strada*, 'Epoca', November 1950; C. BURROW, *Intense Reality–Keynote of sculpture by Marini*, 'New York Herald Tribune', February 1950; J. WATSON CRANE, *Marini's Approach*, 'The Washington Post', March 1950; A. B. LOUCHHEIM, *Marino Marini*, 'The New York Times', 19th February 1950; H. DEVREE, *Marini's Sculpture*, 'The New York Times', 19th February 1950; P. FIERENS, *L'Art Italien au Palais des Beaux-Arts de Bruxelles*, 'Arts', Paris, 3rd February 1950; A. PODESTA, *Situazione Critica di Marini*, 'Emporium', January 1951; J. BERGER, *Drawings by Marino Marini*, 'Signature', 12, London, 1951; G. DI SAN LAZZARO, *Nouveaux destins de l'Art*, 'XX Siècle', Paris, 1951; W. HAFTMANN, *Der bildhauer Marino Marini*, 'Die Kunst', Munich, 1951; G. L. GIOVANOLA, *Marino Marini*, 'Fiera Letteraria', January 1951; M. VALSECCHI, *Uno scultore conquista Londra*, 'Oggi', 7th June 1951; A. PODESTA, *Situazione critica di Marini*, 'Emporium', January 1951; *The sculpture of Marino Marini*, 'Arts et Architecture', New York, June 1951; *Una mostra e un detto di Marino*, 'Domus', Milan, October 1951; M. NETTER, *Marino Marini*, 'Inspiré', April 1951; M. MINASSIAN, *Attualità di Marini*, 'Gazzetta Veneta', Padua, 25th January 1951; M. GASSER, *Besuch bei Marino Marini*, 'Die Neue Zeitung', Berlin, 21st October 1951; F. BELLONZI, *Un erede del Rinascimento in America*, 'La Fiera Letteraria', 2nd September 1951; F. RASCHE, *Der bildhauer Marino Marini*, 'Hannoverversche Zeitung', 24th November 1951; H. TH. FLEMMING, *Der bildhauer Marino Marini*, 'Süddeutsche Zeitung', 30th November 1951; W. HAFTMANN, *Massive und krause Form*, 'Die Zeit', Hamburg, 29th November 1951; A. BUESCHE, *Marini plastik in Hannover*, 'Der Tagesspiegel', 27th November 1951; W. SCHLUTER, *Erste deutsche Ausstellung Marino Marini in der Kenstnergesellschaft*, 'Norddeutsche Zeitung', Hanover, 28th November 1951; M., *Marino Marini breugt Kort bezock aan ous land*, 'De Tiyo', Amsterdam, 30th November 1951; W. MATTHES, *Marino Marini*, 'Frankfurter Allgemeine Zeitung', 27th November 1951; J. FRERKING, *Marino Marini*, 'Allgemeine Zeitung', 27th November 1951; G. MERGLER, *Der Bildhauer Marino Marini*, 'Stuttgarter Nachrichten', 1st December 1951; M. GASSER, *Fantastische en gedeformeerde figuren van gips*, 'Zadertag', Amsterdam, 10th November 1951; M. TAPIÈ, *Un Art Autre*, Paris, 1952; *Marino Marini*, 'Konstrevy', Stockholm, 1952; H. LIST, *Marino Marini*, 'Die Kunst', Munich, April 1952; W. HAFTMANN, *Marino Marini*, 'Das Kunstwerk', Baden-Baden, 1952; *Marino Marini*, 'World Review', London, June 1952; *Nouvelles Conceptions de l'Espace*, 'XX Siècle', Paris, January 1952; *Art et Poésie depuis Apollinaire*, 'XX Siècle', Paris, June 1952; U. DIAMARE, *La scultura*, 'Le arti', June 1952; N. JACOMETTI, *La XXVI Biennale*, 'Art Documents', Geneva, October 1952; G. L. GIOVANOLA, *Giro d'orizzonte sulla scultura italiana*, 'La Fiera Letteraria', Rome, 22nd June 1952; G. DORFLES, *Modern Sculpture in Italy*, 'The Studio', October 1952; M. VALSECCHI, *Rifiutato a Milano–Onorato a Stoccolma*, 'Oggi', 25th December 1952; E. CARLI, *Marino Marini*, 'Emporium', July–August 1952; F. N., *Marino Marini in München*, 'Süddentsche Zeitung', 23rd March 1952; B. DEGENHART, *Der Bildhauer Marino Marini*, 'Die Presse', Vienna, 19th April 1952; L. BORGESE, *La raffinatezza formale dello scultore Marini*, 'Corriere della Sera', Milan, 16th September 1952; G. OTTANI, *Marino Marini*, 'Azione', Lugano, September 1952; U. APOLLONIO, *Marino*, 'La Biennale di Venezia', page 35, July 1952; L. ANCESCHI, *Appunti sulla XXVI Biennale*, 'Gazzetta di Bergamo', August 1952; M. SAWIN, *Marino Marini*, 'Art Digest', New York, 1st November 1953; K. HJERN, *Marino Marini*, 'Konstrevy Hefte', page 20, Stockholm, 1953; T. BERGMARK, Omkring Marini, 'Paletten', I, Göteborg, 1953; U. GERTZ, *Plastik der Gegenwart*, 'Rembrandt Verlag', Berlin, 1953; M. VALSECCHI, *La Scultura di Marino*, 'L'Illustrazione Italiana', Milan, January 1953; E. TRIER, *Mailänder Skizzen*, 'Freie Welt', Cologne, 3rd December 1953; SINAGRA, *Marino Marini a New York*, 'Domus', December 1953; R. REVOLD, *Marino Marini*, 'Kunsten Idag', I, Oslo, 1953; H. DEVREE, *Modern Background–Marini*, 'The New York Times', November 1953; *Sculpture by Marini*, 'New York Herald Tribune', 1st November 1953; M. GASSER, *Junge Italiener*, 'Die Weltwoche', Zurich, 27th November 1953; G. BALLO, *Marini ha vinto puntando sui propri cavalli*, 'Settimo giorno', 22nd August 1953; E. G., *Sculpture by Marini*, 'New York Herald Tribune', 1st November 1953; B. IDELIUS, *Marini*, 'Aftonposten', Göteborg, 16th January 1953; R. ANDERBERG, *Marino Marini*, 'Göteborgsposten', 30th January 1953; G. A., *Hästarna är Minteater sade glad Marino Marini*, 'Ny Tid-Torsdagen', 5th February 1953; R. JOSEPHSON, *Marino Marini*, 'Svenska Dagbladet', Stockholm, 11th February 1953; L. E. ASTROM, *Hästen och ryttaren*, 'Lördagen', 14th February 1953; N. PALMGREN, *Marini*, 'Aftonbladet', 24th February 1953; G. JOHANSSON, *Marini*, 'Svenska Dagbladet', 15th February 1953; A. MEYERSON, *Marino Marini*, 'Morgon Tidningen', Stockholm, 19th February 1953; K. FLOR, *Marino Marini Udstilling paa Kunstmuseet*, 'Berlingske Tidente', Copenhagen, 15th March 1953; S. SCHULTZ, *Marino Marini*, 'Nationaltidente', Copenhagen, 15th March 1953; P. LUBECKER, *Marino Marini*, 'Politiken', Copenhagen, 15th March 1953; T. LINDSTROM, *Marini*, 'Horsens Avis', Copenhagen, 2nd March 1953; H. DHEJNE, *Marini*, 'Sydsvenska Dagblated', 10th March 1953; O. GELSTED, *Kvinder og ryttere*, 'Land og Folk', 26th March 1953; L. ESTVAD, *Rytteren og haus Hest*, 'Skriver', 3rd March 1953; M. M., *Kunstmuseet praesentere Marino Marini*, 'Socialdemokraten', 15th March 1953; T. LINDSTROM, *Vaerker af den italienske Marino Marini forste Gang i Danmark*, 'Korso Avis', 25th March 1953; ID., *Marino Marini forst Gang i Danmark*, 'Kallundborg Avis', 25th March 1953; B. ENGELSTOFT, *Marino Marini udstillingen i Kunstmuseet*, 'Information', Copenhagen, 21st March 1953; O. PARMANN, *Billedhuggeren Marino Marini*, 'Morgenbladet', 25th April 1953; S. STEEN JOHNSEN, *Marino Marini*, 'Dagbladet', 22th April 1953; H. STENSTADVOLD, *Marino Marini*, 'Aftenposten', 22nd April 1953; J. F. MICHELET, *Plastik opplevelse*, 'Verdens Gan', 24th April 1953; J. MOSS, *Marino Marini i Nasjonalgalleriet*, 'Morgenposten', 29th April 1953; *Marino Marini non cederà alla moda*, 'L'Europeo', 7th May 1953; M. NETTER, *Neue Arbeiten von Marino Marini*, 'Werk', Winterthur, April 1954; I. ANDRENIUS, *Marino Marini*, 'Ark', Helsinki, March 1954; E. TRIER, *Moderne Plastik von Rodin bis Marino Marini*, Berlin, 1954; *Ein Plastiker unserer Zeit–Marino Marini*, 'Papagei', Cologne, November 1954; J. P. URGUL, *El escultor Marino Marini*, 'Mundo Uraguayo', Montevideo, 4th March 1954; E. TRIER, *Der bildhauer Marino Marini*, 'Werk und Zeit', Düsseldorf, 1954; M. NETTER, *Lo scultore Marino Marini*, 'Minerva', Turin, May 1954; *Nello studio di Marino*, 'Domus', Milan, August 1954; B. JOPPOLO, *Deux sculpteurs–Marini, Calder*, 'XX siècle', Paris, January 1954; D. FELDENKIRCHEN, *Marino Marini im Spiegel*, 'Kölner Leben', Cologne, June 1954; M. SARFATTI, *Marini e Sironi oggi in America*, 'La Patria', 1st February 1954; E. TRIER, *Marino Marini in Köln*, 'Frankfurter Allgemeine Zeitung', 3rd July 1954; L. VENTURI, *Marino Marini*, 'La Nuova Stampa', 12th June 1954; A. SCHULZE VELLING-HAUSEN, *Marini in Düsseldorf*, 'Frankfurter Allgemeine Zeitung', 26th May 1955; T. VIZIJE, *Susreti's Marinijem*, 'Novine', Belgrade, 15th May 1955; E. TRIER, *Moderne Plastik von Rodin bis Marino Marini*, Büchergilde Gutenberg, Frankfurt am Main, 1955; M. NEGRI, *Marino Marini*, 'Domus', Milan, June 1955; *In un'autorimessa nascono capolavori*, 'Corriere d'Informazioni', Milan, 17th–18th October 1955; R. BEZOMBES, *Marino Marini*, 'Arts', Paris, 5th October 1955; H. REETZ, *Marino Marini in der Mannheimer Kunsthalle*, 'Rheinpfalz', Ludwigshafen, 27th June 1955; U. SEELMANN EGGEBERT, *Zur Ausstelllung der italienischen Bildhauers Marino Marini*, 'Mannheimer Morgen', 25th June 1955; E. A. J., *Marino Marini*, 'Allgemeine Zeitung', Mannheim, 27th June 1955; EGO, *Plastiken und Zeichnungen von Marino Marini*, 'Badische Volkszeitung', Mannheim, 27th June 1955; JEM. LANGUI, *Marino Marini*, 'Het Handelsblad', 31st May 1955; M. GASSER, *Marino Marini in der Werkstatt*, 'Die Weltwoche', Zürich, 10th June 1955; G. VIELHABER, *Giacometti neben Marini, zwei bedeutende Bildhauer der Gegenwart*, 'Die Welt', Düsseldorf, 25th May 1955; R. HAASE, *Marini vollendet archaische Kunst*, 'Neue Rhein Zeitung', 17th May 1955; W. FISCHER, *Marini und Giacometti*, 'Volkszeitung', 21st May 1955; E. TRIER, *Mittelmeerische Plastiker der Zeit*, Hamburg, 2nd June 1955; H. S., *Marino Marini*, 'Freies Volk', 24th May 1955; A. KLAPHECK, *Zwei Bildhauer der Gegenwart*, 'Rheinische Post', 14th May 1955; W. TAMMS, *Der italienische Bildhauer Marini stellt in Düsseldorf aus*, 'Westdeutsche Allgemeine', May 1955; K. S., *Marino Marini in Museum Boymans*, 'Neue Schiedamse Courant', 12th March 1955; H. R. R., *Marino Marini in Museum Boymans*, 'Trouw', Rotterdam, 5th March 1955; C. DOCHMANN, *Marino Marini*, 'Nieuwe Rotterdamse Courant', 5th March 1955; J. VAN DER STER, *Marino Marini*, 'De Groene Amsterdammer', 12th March 1955; A. LAAN, *Ruiters van Marini in Museum Boymans*, 'Het Vrije Volk', 5th March 1955; CH. WENTINCK, *Mensen en dieren van Marini*, 'Elseviers Weekblad', 19th March 1955; *Marino Marini*, 'Nieuwe Rotterdamse Courant', 5th March 1955; B. DEGENHART, *Italienische Zeichner der Gegenwart*, Berlin, 1956; F. RUSSOLI, *Dix ans d'Art Contemporaine '45–'55*, 'XX Siècle', Paris, 1956; H. R. HAHNLOSER, *Werke aus der Sammlung Hahnloser*, 'Du', Zürich, November 1956; E. NEWTON, *Jawlensky and Marini*, 'Time and Tide', London, 12th May 1956; J. HALL, *Marino Marini*, 'Truth', London, May 1956; J. WHEELOCK FREEMAN, *Marino Marini: his work and his home*, 'Esquire', August 1956; M. NEGRI, *Particolari nella scultura di Marino Marini*, 'Domus', Milan, August 1957; TELICHI-HIJKATA, *Scultura Italiana Contemporanea*, Tokyo, 1957; M. MOSCHI, *Marino Marini*, 'La Nazione', Florence, 11th January 1957; W. SCHUMANN, *Marino Marini bei Vömel*, 'Rheinische Post', 26th March 1957; U. BINDER HAGELSTANGE, *Kavalkade in der Kunsthalle Baden-Baden*, 'Frankfurter Allgemeine Zeitung', 12th August 1957; L. ZANUCCO, *una statua equestre de Marini adornerà una piazza dell'Aja*, 'La Nazione', Florence, 29th April 1957; M. L. FUNES, *Marino Marini y el arte figurativo*, Caracas, 29th August 1957; Y. F., *Marino Marini in Hannover*, 'Frankfurter Allgemeine Zeitung', 9th November 1957; U. APOLLONIO, *Marino Marini*, 'Prisme', 15, Paris, 1958; W. HOFMANN, *Die Plastik des 20. Jahrhunderts*, Fischer Bücherei, Frankfurt am Main, 1958; M. LUZ, *Peintures de Marino Marini*, 'XX Siècle', Paris, March 1958; *Het Kolossale paard van Marino Marini*, 'Zaderdag', 4th January 1958; S. PRESTON, *Italian Contemporaries–Marini*, 'The New York Times Sunday', 16th March 1958; R. E. PENNING, *Ruiter van Marini onthuld*, 'Haagsche Courant', 2nd May 1959; C. B. ASOSKI, *Het Paard van Marini als Teken des Tijd*, 'Neiuwe Haagsche Courant', 2nd May 1959; R. E. PENNING, *Gesprek met Marini*, 'Haagsche Courant', 1st May 1959; E. RODITI, *Pferd, Reiter und die Katastrophe*, 'Der Monat', Berlin, April 1959; TETSNO ABE, *Marino Marini, Looking at Europe*, 'Forefront of Art', Tokyo, November 1959; F. RUSSOLI, *Un cavaliere di Marino Marini*, 'Arte Oggi', Milan, June 1959; M. VALSECCHI, *A Firenze toccai la barba di Rodin*, 'Il Giorno', Milan, 8th September 1959; E. RODITI, *Changing the Horse–Marino Marini*, 'The Observer', 17th April 1960; E. GOPEL, *Besuch bei dem Bildhauer Marino Marini in Mailand*, 'Frankfurter Allgemeine Zeitung', 4th October 1960; G. C., *Marino Marini*, 'Graphis', 91, Zürich, 1960; F. RUSSOLI, *Gli ultimi cavalieri di Marino*, 'Arte Figurative', Milan, May–June 1960; E. RODITI, *Marino Marini*, 'The Observer', 17th April 1960; E. TRIER, *La tragica scultura di Marini*, 'Arte Club', June–August 1961; M. LEEB HADZI, *Whit Marino Marini*, 'World of Art', v. 49, New York; R. BERGER, *Persistance de l'humain*, 'XX Siècle', Paris, 1961; *Monumento di Marino Marini all'Aja*, 'Domus', February 1961; E. PREIFFER-BELLI, *Tragische Monumentalität zum Werk des bildhauers Marino Marini*, 'Das Schönste', Munich, June 1961; E. GOPEL, *Besuch bei Marino Marini*, 'Weltkunst', Munich, April 1961; G. LIVI, *Marino Marini–La vita segreta di un grande scultore*, 'Epoca', Milan, 15th October

1961; J. CHAMPOMIER, *Marino Marini*, 'La Dépeche', Clermond Ferrand, 18th October 1961; M. MOSCHI, *Lo scultore Marino Marini alla Mostra di piazza Donatello*, 'La Nazione', Florence, 8th September 1961; F. NEMITZ, *Marino Marini zum 60. Geburtstag des italienischen Bildhauers*, 'Süddentsche Zeitung', 27th February 1961; H. PLATTE, *Marino Marini–zwei Reiter*, Monatshefte Vestermann Verlag, October 1962; D. SCHMIDT, *Stationen im Werk Marino Marinis*, 'Die Kunst', Munich, May 1962; M. VALSECCHI, *I cavalieri disarcionati*, 'L'Illustrazione Italiana', Milan, March 1962; G. CARANDENTE, *Sculture nella città*, Spoleto, December 1962; G. PEILLEX, *Marino Marini a Zurigo*, 'Le Arti', 2, February 1962; R. TASSI, *Nei 'cavalieri' di Marino Marini l'Etruria ha incontrato la Cina*, 'Settimo Giorno', Milan, 13th February 1962; G., *Der Bildhauer Marino Marini in Zürcher Kunsthaus*, 'Sie und Er', 24, Zürich, 25th January 1962; E. FABIANI, *Per lui la vita è un cavallo bizzarro*, 'Gente', Rome, 23rd February 1962; A. K., *La sculpture de Marino Marini*, 'La Gazette de Lausanne', 6th–7th January 1962; L. CARAMEL, *Marino Marini*, 'Arte Lombarda', VI, 2, 1962; F. BILLETER, *Die Gesamtschau von Marino Marini in Zürcher Kunsthaus*, 'Zürcher Woche', 2nd February 1962; R. S., *Marino Marini im Kunsthaus*, 'Wolksrecht', 3rd February 1962; H. GR., *Marino Marini*, 'Neue Zürcher Nachrichten', Zürich, 29th January 1962; H. R. HALLER, *Erstante Tragikomödie Marino Marini*, 'Schweizer Familien Wochenblatt', Zürich, 17th February 1962; F. L., *Marino Marini oder das Ende des Helden*, 'Tages Anzeiger', Kanton Zürich, 26th January 1962; P. E., *Marino Marini*, 'Luzerner Tagblatt', Lucerne, 27th January 1962; G. R., *Marino Marini ein Zeitgenössicher italienischer Meister*, 'Zürichsee Zeitung', 30th January 1962; K. SPEICH, *Marino Marini zum Ausstellung im Kunsthaus Zürich*, 'Neues Winterthurer Tagblatt', 27th January 1962; F. BILLETER, *Ein interview mit Marino Marini*, 'Zürcher Woche', Zürich, 26th January 1962; E. GUREWITSCH, *Marini–Sculpture reflects tragedy of today*, 'Weekly Tribune', Geneva, 2nd February 1962; H. DANNECKER, *Der Urplastiker–Marino Marini*, 'Schwäbische Zeitung', 27th January 1962; D. SCHMIDT, *Der Bildhauer Marino Marini*, 'Süddeutsche Zeitung', 26th January 1962; H. KINKEL, *Marini*, 'Stuttgarter Zeitung', 25th January 1962; W. JONAS, *Marino Marini im Kunsthaus*, 'Die Tat', Zürich, 27th January 1962; A. P., *Marino Marini le sculpteur du 'Miracle'*, 'Feuille D'Avis de Neuchatel', 17th February 1962; M. VALSECCHI, *Cosa fa Milano per i massimi scultori di oggi?*, 'Il Giorno', Milan, 2nd February 1962; O. OBOUSSIER, *Marino Marini in Zürcher Kunsthaus*, 'Aargauer Tagblatt', 10th February 1962; W. WESTECKER, *Marino Marini–Plastik ist tragische Architektur*, 'Christ und Welt', Stuttgart, 9th March 1962; E. G. GUREWITSCH, *Marini's Horses of Armageddon*, 'The Christian Science Monitor', New York, 12th March 1962; P. K. WEHRLI, *M. Marini–Untergang im Narren kleid*, 'Zolliker Bote', Zollikon, 16th March 1962; M. GASSER, *Marino Marini*, 'Die Weltwoche', Zürich, 26th January 1962; R. HASLI, *Marino Marini, Eine Ausstellung im Kunsthaus Zürich*, 'Neue Zürcher Zeitung', Zürich, 26th January 1962; H. W. PETZET, *Mirakel der schrecklichen Pferde*, 'Deutsche Zeitung', 30th January 1962; P. K. WEHRLI, *Marino Marini–Harlekin am Abgrund*, 'Schaffhausen Nachrichten', 23rd March 1962; C. L. RAGGHIANTI, *Marini*, 'Sele Arte', Ivrea, January–February 1963; M. GASSER, *Der Porträtist Marino Marini*, 'Du', Zürich, October 1963; M. VALSECCHI, *I giovani mi aiutano a capire il mondo d'oggi*, 'Tempo', Milan, 2nd December 1963; R. CARRIERI, *Ecco il fantastico circo di Marini*, 'Europeo', Milan, December 1963; F. RUSSOLI, *Le Guerrier de Marino Marini*, 'XX Siècle', Paris, May 1963; A. SORELLI, *Marino Marini*, 'L'Informatore Moderno', 26th May 1963; L. BORGESE, *Marino Marini*, 'Corriere della Sera', Milan, 22nd December 1963; D. ADLOW, *Marini*, 'The Christian Science Monitor', Boston, 13th December 1963; M. D. M., *Marino Marini*, 'L'Unità', Rome, 14th December 1963; W. CHRISTLIEB, *Ein Bildhauer der sich als Maler stellt: Marino Marini*, 'Epoca', Milan, 2nd April 1964; M. M., *Marino: ritratto di Arp*, 'Domus', Milan, 1964; H. READ, *Modern Sculpture*, New York, 1964; J. P. HODIN, *Marino Marini*, 'The Studio', London, March 1964; R. BARLETTA, *Marino Marini e il cavaliere nell'arte*, 'Letteratura', Rome, January–April 1964; M. NOZZA, *Marino Marini–L'ispirazione al Galoppo*, 'L'Europeo', Milan, 30th August 1964; V. DEL GAIZO, *Marino Marini grafico e pittore*, 'Fiera Europea', June 1964; O. PATANI, *Marino Marini*, 'Arti figurative', Milan, February 1964; *I dipinti di Marino Marini*, 'Domus', Milan, February 1964; E. RODITI, *Cavalier Apocalyptiques*, 'La Revue de Paris', October 1964; F. RUSSOLI, *Marino Marini*, 'Libri e Riviste d'Italia', Rome, June 1964; *Marino Marini als schilder*, 'Nieuwe Rotterdamse Courant', 14th November 1964; A. BOSMAN, *Marino Marini even goed schilder als beeldhouwer*, 'Algemeen Dagblad', 13th November 1964; E. PFEIFFER-BELLI, *Dreissig Werke von Marino Marini*, 'Die Welt', Munich, 15th May 1964; A. BOVI, *Colore e forma nella pittura di Marino Marini*, 'Il Messaggero', Rome, 13th January 1964; P. C. SANTINI, *Marino Marini pittore. Esplora nei quadri la sua scultura*, 'L'Espresso', 1st March 1964; M. R., *C'è un rapporto drammatico fra uomo e cavallo–La scoperta di un Marini pittore*, 'Avanti', Milan, 28th January 1964; W. PUFF, *Von Uccello zu Marini*, 'Maske und Metapher', Nuremberg, 1965; J. P. HODIN, *Noodelijke nostalgie en Etruskische erfenis*, 'Kronich van Kunst en Kultuur', Amsterdam, September 1965; F. RUSSOLI, *Marino Marini–Il guerriero*, 'Il Poliedro', 8, January 1965; L. PAPI, *Guardano a Firenze i cavalli di Marino*, 'La Nazione', Florence, 16th October 1965; L. CARLUCCIO, *Pensosi cavalieri e cavalli gremiscono i ritorni in Versilia di Marino Marini*, 'Gazzetta del Popolo', Turin, 31st August 1965; M. FAGIOLO, *L'Opera di Marino Marini dall'apocalisse all'ironia*, 'Avanti', 18th July 1965; R. D. C., *Marino Marini als schilder*, 'Het Volk', 3rd March 1965; B. L., *82 peintures du sculpteur toscan Marino Marini sur quelques thèmes fondamentaux*, 'La Metropole', 4th March 1965; R. DE CNODDER, *Marino Marini als Schilder in Konstmuseum*, 'Toonel', Antwerp, 5th March 1965; L. BEKKERS, *Marino Marini*, 'De Nieuwe', 5th March 1965; D. GRAFLY, *Persuasive Sense of Power Found in Marini Exhibition*, 'Book and Art', Philadelphia, 12th December 1965; V. DONOHOE, *Exhibit of Italy's Top Artist*, 'The Philadelphia Inquirer', 12th December 1965; F. LUDOVISI, *Cavalli e Donne di Marino Marini a Palazzo Venezia*, 'Le Ore', Rome, 24th March 1966; F. L. LIVI, *Galoppano su Roma i cavalli di Marino*, 'Arianna', Milan, March 1966; P. BRUZZI-CHELLI, *Marino Marini e il suo Miracolo*, 'Rocca', 7, April 1966; C. L. RAGGHIANTI,

Marino, 'SeleArte', Ivrea, January–June 1966; M. VENTUROLI, *Marino Marini*, 'D'ars Agency', March–April 1966; A. PICA, *Marino Marini in Palazzo Venezia*, 'Domus', Milan, September 1966; G. MARUSSI, *Marino Marini a Palazzo Venezia*, 'Le Arti', Milan, February 1966; E. ADELMANN, M. CONIL LACOSTE, *Europäische Plastik der Gegenwart*, Stuttgart, 1966; *Marino Marini Reiterbilder*, 'Die Kunst', Munich, February 1966; M. VALSECCHI, *Marini documenta il nostro tempo*, 'Tempo', Milan, 23rd March 1966; L. TRUCCHI, G. MONTESANTO, *Marino Marini etrusco fedele*, 'La Fiera Letteraria', 24th March 1966; *Incontro con Marino*, 'La Fiera Letteraria', 24th March 1966; G. MASCHERPA, *Un mago etrusco a Palazzo Venezia*, 'Gente', Rome, 16th March 1966; M. VENTUROLI, *Lo scultore Marino Marini fra Italia ed Europa*, 'Le Ore', 10th February 1966; R. BIASON, *Marini e i suoi cavalli hanno fatto moltissima strada*, 'Oggi', Milan, 7th April 1966; *Marino Marini's Lusty Art*, 'Time', Atlantic edition, 27th May 1966; H. KIEL, *Marino Marini*, 'Die Kunst und das Schöne Heim', Munich, March 1966; G. MARUSSI, *Il mondo poetico di Marino Marini*, 'La Nuova Tribuna', April 1966; M. CAMILUCCI, *Marino Marini a Palazzo Venezia*, 'Persona', Rome, April 1966; M. BERTOLDI, *Sono un etrusco che viaggia il mondo*, 'Oggi', Milan, 15th December 1966; SK., *Marino Marini als Maler und Graphiker*, 'Nürnberger Zeitung', 5th September 1966; W. FENN, *Ausstellung mit zweihundert Blättern Marino Marini in der Fränkischen Galerie*, 'Nürnberger Nachrichten', 5th September 1966; W. MOGGE, *Marino Marini als Maler und Grafiker*, 'Saarbrücker Landeszeitung', 9th September 1966; E. M. DEMISCH, *Bildhauer Marino Marini als Maler und Graphiker*, 'Frankfurter Allgemeine Zeitung', July 1966; U. URBINATI, *La Mostra di Marino Marini a Roma*, 'Corriere del Ticino', Lugano, 7th June 1966; M. BERNARDI, *Marino Marini il più famoso e discusso degli scultori italiani*, 'La Stampa', Turin, 23rd March 1966; V. GUZZI, *Veneri, cavalli e mostri nelle sale di Palazzo Venezia*, 'Il Tempo', 11th March 1966; G. VISENTINI, *Inaugurati ieri a Palazzo Venezia una mostra antologica di Marino Marini*, 'Il Messaggero', Rome, 11th March 1966; G. M., *Marino Marini a Palazzo Venezia*, 'La Fiera Letteraria', Rome, 17th March 1966; V. MARIANI, *Il canto desolato di un grande maestro*, 'Il Giornale d'Italia', 9th–10th March 1966; A. PODESTA, *Omaggio a Marino Marini, un grande del nostro tempo*, 'Il Secolo XIX', 12th March 1966; L. PAPI, *Marino Marini a Roma per la sua grande mostra*, 'La Nazione', Florence, 6th March 1966; D. MICACCHI, *L'uomo antico di Marino Marini*, 'L'Unità', 12th March 1966; L. TRUCCHI, *A Palazzo Venezia duecento opere di Marini*, 'Momento Sera', 13th March 1966; A. DRAGONE, *Nelle sculture di Marino Marini un drammatico sigillo della nostra età*, 'Stampa Sera', Turin, 11th March 1966; O. OBRY, *L'Homme à cheval au Palazzo Venezia ou la consécration de Marino Marini*, 'Combat', Paris, 13th April 1966; Y. SCHMITZ VAN VORST, *Der angeklagte Marino Marini*, 'Frankfurter Allgemeine Zeitung', 25th April 1966; G. BRIGANTI, *Sorrisi etruschi su volti moderni–La Mostra di Marino Marini*, 'Expresso', 27th March 1966; L. BORGESE, *Marini dal gotico al cinese*, 'Il Corriere della Sera', Milan, 8th April 1966; L. TALLARICO, *Marino Marini un etrusco moderno*, 'Il Secolo d'Italia', 29th March 1966; A. DRAGONE, *Marino Marini artista etrusco*, 'Il nostro Tempo', 27th March 1966; S. GAUDIO, *La vita operosa di Marino Marini*, 'Il Dovere', Bellinzona, 29th April 1966; M. VALSECCHI, *Ha scavato negli uomini la sua scultura*, 'Il Giorno', Milan, 10th March 1966; P. WALDO SCHWARTZ, *Marini Dialogue with Humanity*, 'The New York Times', International Edition, 8th March 1966; J. SILLECK, *New Reality for Marini*, 'Daily American', Rome, 7th March 1966; G. GIUFFRÈ, *Nota su Marino Marini scultore*, 'Arte Sintesi', May–August 1966; A. BALLIS, *Marini–'Devo qualcosa a Rodin'*, 'Il Gazzettino', Venice, 30th March 1967; J. ROH, *Marino Marini–Pferd mit Gauklern*, 'Westermanns Monatshefte', 1967; M. VALSECCHI, *Di Marino Marini la 'Donnina di Milano'*, 'Il Corriere della Sera', Milan, 28th October 1967; BO BOUSTEDT, *Vivre avec la Siècle*, Paris, June 1967; N. ANDREINA GALLI, *Con Marino Marini–Un uomo di genio, cittadino del mondo*, 'La Nazione', Florence, 6th August 1967; F. LICHT, *Sculpture 19th and 20th Centuries*, 'A History of Western Sculpture', London, 1967; L. PICCIONI, *Marino Marini si sente straniero in Italia*, 'Tempo', Milan, 29th August 1967; G. LINDEMANN, *Kunst, Künstler, Kunstwerke, Malerei*, Essen, 1967; F. REGGIORI, *L'Arte Moderna*, Milan, December 1967; D. BUZZATI, *Marino Marini*, 'Il Corriere della Sera', Milan, 28th October 1967; BO BOUSTEDT, *Vivre avec la sculpture*, 'XX Siècle', Paris, December 1967; *Marino*, 'L'Espresso', 5th November 1967; M. CALABRESE, *Marino Marini*, 'Il Poliedro', Rome, November 1967; V. MOLTER, *Liebe strömtLeben aus*, 'Feuilleton', Munich, 12th October 1967; F. LICHT, *Sculpture 19th and 20th Centuries*, London 1967; F. PICCININI, *Marino Marini ci parla di sé e degli altri*, 'Fatti', Milan, 16th–23rd February 1968; C. L. RAGGHIANTI, *Marino Marini a Firenze*, 'La Nazione', Florence, 12th April 1968; A. BONSANTI, *Una frase e un gesto*, 'La Nazione', Florence, 12th April 1968; L. PAPI, *I suoi cavalli*, 'La Nazione', Florence, 12th April 1968; *Marino Marini a Firenze*, 'Giornale del Popolo', Lugano, 18th April 1968; C. PIROVANO, *Scultura Italiana*, Milan, 1968; P. F. LISTRI, *L'Apocalisse di Marino*, 'La Nazione', Florence, 23rd May 1968; ID., *Pascoleranno in Boboli i cavalli di Marino*, 'La Fiera Letteraria', Milan, 30th May 1968; P. SPIGARELLI, *L'opera di Marino Marini tradotta nelle foto*, 'Il Lavoro', Pistoia, 8th June 1968; *Marino Marini alla vernice delle sur opere fotografiche*, 'La Nazione', 8th June 1968; P. SPIGARELLI, *In quaranta pannelli le opere di Marino Marini*, 'Il Lavoro', Pistoia, 9th June 1968; G. SAVINO, *'Le calde immagini' della scultura di Marini*, 'La Nazione', Florence, 13th June 1968; M. MARINI, *De la couleur à la forme–Panorama '68*, 'XX Siècle', Paris, 30th June 1968; M. VALSECCHI, *Incontro con Marino Marini*, 'Il Giorno', Milan, 13th July 1968.